40
YEARS
OF
Chez Panisse

40 YEARS OF Chez Panisse

THE POWER OF GATHERING

ALICE WATERS
AND FRIENDS

Foreword by Calvin Trillin | *Afterword by Michael Pollan*

CLARKSON POTTER/PUBLISHERS

NEW YORK

 For all the cooks of Chez Panisse

Grateful acknowledgment is made to Yale University Press and John Hollander for permission to reprint "A Watched Pot" from *Types of Shape: New, Expanded Edition* by John Hollander, copyright © 1967, 1968, 1969, 1991 by John Hollander.

Photograph credits appear on page 301.

Published in the United States by Clarkson Potter/Publishers, an imprint of the CrownPublishing Group, a division of Random House, Inc., New York.
www.crownpublishing.com
www.clarksonpotter.com

CLARKSON POTTER is a trademark and POTTER with colophon is a registered trademark of Random House, Inc.

Library of Congress Cataloging-in-Publication Data is available upon request.

ISBN 978-0-307-71826-6
eISBN 978-0-307-95336-0

Printed in the United States of America

Design by Malgosia Szemberg
Calligraphy by Lauren McIntosh

10 9 8 7 6 5 4 3 2 1

First Edition

Contents

Foreword by Calvin Trillin

CALVIN TRILLIN (*writer*): I once referred to Alice Waters as the Emma Goldman of the New American Cuisine. She's a revolutionary, and I have to believe that her revolutionary approach was affected by what was happening at the University of California at Berkeley when she arrived there as an undergraduate in the sixties. I was in Berkeley not long after Alice arrived; I had come to do a piece on the Free Speech Movement for *The New Yorker*. I found that the student radicals I met had a style (a word they used a lot) that was militantly inclusive and nonhierarchical. The organization they most admired, the Student Nonviolent Coordinating Committee, which provided the young shock troops for the civil rights struggle in the South, was said to make decisions by "letting the consensus emanate." Before the Berkeley radicals got deflected and eventually consumed by the Vietnam War, they were interested in organizing around issues that were specific and close at hand—a rent strike in substandard housing in Oakland, say, or working conditions on the farms of the Central Valley. If their interests had been culinary rather than political, they would have been locavores.

In those days, when good food was intertwined in the American mind with "fine dining," the style of leading restaurants was neither inclusive nor nonhierarchical nor local. The chef was a magisterial figure in a towering toque. The menu needed but a single word to designate the high quality of an ingredient—*imported*. The waiters wore tuxedos and the maître d' seemed to have been hired for his ability to make patrons feel that they didn't quite deserve to be on the premises. Every middle-size American city had a couple of versions of this restaurant.

I called it La Maison de la Casa House, Continental Cuisine and speculated that the continent they had in mind was Antarctica, where everything starts out frozen.

Chez Panisse was instrumental in overthrowing that regime. It uncoupled good eating from fanciness. Its menu included takes on humble street food, like pizza and calzone. It hired the sort of chefs who wore baseball caps rather than toques and might have found themselves drifting into kitchen work after getting bored with graduate studies in anthropology. It was wildly inclusive. The growers were an honored part of the operation. The customers knew they deserved to be on the premises and didn't seem to mind that Alice was serving up, with the heirloom tomatoes and free-range chicken, some strong views on the connection between good food and sustainable agriculture. Now, every middle-size American city has a couple of restaurants that are modeled, in one way or another, on Chez Panisse. Like any good radical, Alice seemed interested from the start in creating not an empire but a network.

I tend to eat in the upstairs café at Chez Panisse rather than in the more formal dining room downstairs, but I find it comforting to know that the dining room is there. Why? Because for fifteen years, beginning in the late sixties, I was in a strange town every three weeks for a series of *New Yorker* pieces, and my last resort for finding something decent to eat was to approach the motel clerk and say, "Not the restaurant you took your parents to on their twenty-fifth wedding anniversary; the restaurant you went to the night you got home after thirteen months in Korea." In Berkeley, I'm pleased to say, those are the same restaurant.

I would like to invite you to share a personal and impressionistic chronicle of the evolution of a small restaurant and café in Berkeley, California, called Chez Panisse.

An Introduction and an Invitation by Alice Waters

To put this history together, first my collaborators and I pored over thousands of photographs, menus, and other ephemera, looking for memorable images that would be expressive enough to tell the story all by themselves. After we had arranged the pictures in more or less chronological order, and after I had written about what they meant to me, I invited nearly a hundred friends to contribute their recollections, too. Regrettably, hundreds more friends of the restaurant who have also been indispensable members of the Panisse family have been left out; and without their stories, this book can only be fragmentary, incomplete, and subjective. But in the end the only story I can tell is my own. So here it is: my story, mostly in pictures; the story of what I have learned and how the restaurant has come to flourish.

For decades, Chez Panisse has been serving its guests not just food, but ideas. The real story of this book is how a few simple ideas about food and culture—ideas that are accessible to anyone—were planted in my mind before the restaurant was founded and became convictions that took root, blossomed, and bore fruit, to be propagated from Berkeley back out into the world.

What are these ideas we've been serving? They are neither new nor radical. In fact, they are as old as humankind. Most important is the universal idea that we have an obligation to support the farmers, fishermen, and ranchers who are taking care of the planet at the same time they are nourishing us, and an equally solemn obligation to nourish our children, who are depending on us for a livable future. Another idea is that our full humanity is contingent on our hospitality: we can be complete only when we are giving something away; when we sit at the table and pass the peas to the person next to us we see that person in a whole new way. Finally, and critically, we've been serving forth the idea that the whole is greater than the sum of its parts. This concept explains, among other things, how a restaurant like Chez Panisse becomes not just a place to eat, but also a convivial venue for celebrating and savoring particular moments in time, a forum for political engagement, and an ongoing opportunity for artistic collaboration.

Our vision at Chez Panisse has always been of a world where delicious food enriches the celebration of life and strengthens our connections to nature and culture. To turn this vision into reality, we need to gather together at the table and prove that the authenticity we crave can exist right under our noses. This is the power of gathering: it inspires us—delightfully—to be more hopeful, more joyful, more thoughtful: in a word, more alive.

To me, a Greek theater is a transcendent cultural space, a stage in nature where we can assemble as a community. Here, in the William Randolph Hearst Greek Theater at the University of California at Berkeley, is where I first learned that people could gather under one sky and change the world.

Alice Waters *(center, looking at camera)* at a sixties antiwar protest.

1964
Berkeley

the power of gathering

This is a Free Speech Movement rally at the University of California at Berkeley in 1964. I am somewhere in this crowd. I had transferred as a sophomore from Santa Barbara just a few months before and found a university in a state of upheaval. It was an unbelievably stimulating time, and I stumbled right into it—a little uneasy, at the fringe of the movement, a little afraid of committing myself to what I believed, but gradually getting pulled in by the passionate eloquence of its charismatic leader, Mario Savio. I absorbed his idealism and his conviction that people are more than cogs in the machine. He made me believe that my generation could unite to bring about a new world, that we could stop feeling alienated and competitive and instead join together in a righteous cause. In one memorable speech he said, "America is becoming ever more the utopia of sterilized, automated contentment," and hearing this would later help give me the courage to search for a contentment that was unsterilized and fertile and handmade, a contentment that I would find a few years later in the kitchen, a contentment that would last my entire life.

"Your own history was lying in pieces on the ground, and you had the choice of picking up the pieces or passing them by." Greil Marcus

GREIL MARCUS *(music critic, historian, and director, Pagnol et Cie., Inc., the corporation that runs the Chez Panisse restaurant and café)*: In many ways the story of Chez Panisse begins at the University of California at Berkeley in 1964, not long after Alice Waters, late of New Jersey, transferred there from Santa Barbara as a twenty-year-old sophomore. Throughout the spring, students organized demonstrations—picket marches and sit-ins against racial discrimination in hiring practices at businesses in San Francisco and the East Bay. In 1964, if you walked into a branch of the Bank of America, the bank that dominated the Bay Area, you would never see a single teller, agent, or manager who was not white.

Businesses complained to the university. When the fall semester began, the university announced a campus ban on political organizing: on speech, spoken or written, meant to encourage others to take certain actions, or refrain from others. Students deliberately violated the order; the university had them arrested. Within days, the Free Speech Movement took shape—and the result was weeks, then months, of speeches, rallies, discussions, marches, sit-ins, meetings, more rallies, more speeches, more sit-ins. In one way or another, everyone took part. "I came here to go to business school," one friend said—he couldn't have been less interested in politics, in questions of how and why people make judgments about the ordering of their shared shape and time, on what counts and what doesn't according to those judgments—"and all we ever do is talk about this goddamned FSM!"

It was three months of unfettered doubt, chaos, anger, hesitation, confusion, and joy: a sense of freedom. Your own history—such once abstract or distant things as the First Amendment, maybe a line from the Gettysburg Address—was lying in pieces on the ground, and you had the choice of picking up the pieces or passing them by. In this atmosphere, where a school became a terrain on which all emotions, all ideas and theories, were tested and fought over, nothing was trivial, nothing was incidental.

Everything was part of a totality, and that totality was, finally, how you wanted to live.

On December 2, 1964, during the final FSM sit-in on the Berkeley campus—an event that led to the arrest of nearly eight hundred demonstrators, a student strike that shut down the university, and finally the restoration of free speech on the campus—Mario Savio, the most visible speaker of the Free Speech Movement, gave a talk he called "An End to History." "The university," he said, "is the place where people begin seriously to question the conditions of their existence and raise the issue of whether they can be committed to the society they have been born into. After a long period of apathy during the fifties, students have begun not only to question but, having arrived at answers, to act on those answers. This is part of a growing understanding among many people in America that history has not ended, that a better society is possible, and that it is worth dying for."

More than anything else, it was Mario Savio's words that convinced Alice that she, in her own way, had to change the world. Like thousands of other students, she absorbed both Savio's words and the events they described—demonstrations one watched, demonstrations in which one took part, speeches one listened to, speeches one made, to crowds of hundreds or an audience of one, two, or the mirror. There was the notion that one could make one's own history; over the next six years, the nation itself would be convulsed by it. It might take the shape of huge demonstrations against racial injustice, against the Vietnam War—but in a way it was nothing more, and nothing less, than people refusing to accept that history was over, and insisting that the story they would leave behind would be one they told themselves. "If you don't like the news," Scoop Nisker of KSAN-FM in San Francisco liked to say in the years after the Free Speech Movement, "go out and make some of your own," and people took him at his word. "This little place," Mario Savio said in wonderment, "had become one of the central places on the planet."

Mario Savio is dragged from the stage of the Greek Theater after being refused permission to speak by the president of the university. Moments later he was allowed to return. The Free Speech Movement achieved its goal: students at the university were given the right to organize politically. But the turmoil of the sixties didn't subside. The escalation of the war in Vietnam and the rise of the counterculture were still to come.

another kind of

I had never been out of the country before when I decided to study abroad in the winter of 1965. My friend Sara Flanders and I arrived in Paris, and it was like magic to me. I was supposed to be taking a *cours de civilisation* at the Sorbonne, but I hardly ever went to class. I was too busy soaking up the civilization in other ways—sitting in cafés, listening to concerts, arguing about politics—but mostly by eating. From the student cafeteria (that's my meal card, on the left), to restaurants, to the market on rue Mouffetard (*opposite*)—I ate so many things I had never tasted before. I began to appreciate how food anchored life to the land and to the seasons, and I began to dream of sharing all this with my friends back in Berkeley.

France changed my life forever. When I returned to Berkeley in 1966 to finish college, I knew I wanted to live the way my French friends did. These were people who thought of good food as an indispensable part of life, for whom each day was punctuated by food-related decisions. It went without saying that one had to get to the bakery early, to get a fresh, hot baguette; naturally, one spent an hour or so in the afternoon in a café with one's friends; and of course one only bought produce in season, because that's when it was least expensive and tasted best. Eating together was the most important daily ritual in their lives, a crucial and nonnegotiable time when the flavors and smells of roasted chickens and sizzling garlic, the crunch of crusty bread, and the taste of local wine drew out everyone's most passionate ideas and feelings.

Back in California, although I still hadn't imagined a life in a restaurant, I began to cook more and more. I befriended Gene Opton, the owner of a wonderful cooking equipment store in Berkeley called The Kitchen, and she introduced me to the books of Elizabeth David, one of the very greatest writers about food of the twentieth—or any—century. She understood exactly what it takes to eat well: an unrelenting emphasis on quality; an attentive, inquisitive palate; an insistence on eating locally; and (in her words), "learning the art, or the discipline, call it which you like, of leaving well alone."

When I graduated in 1967 I wasn't at all sure what I wanted to do, so naturally I went back to school. In my senior year I had been student teaching at the Montessori School in Berkeley, and that had made me think I should train as a Montessori teacher. The best place to do that back then was at the Maria Montessori Training Organization on Lyndhurst Terrace in London, England, and in the fall of 1968, that's where I headed.

I rented a tiny freezing garret in the tower of an old Victorian neo-medieval house near Hampstead Heath, with two little underpowered Victorian gas burners, a minuscule broiler underneath, and no oven. I was happy

REVOLUTION

awakening to the kindness of strangers and to a new world of beauty and meaning, educating the senses, beginning to understand my place in the world…

Traveling through Turkey and Greece, I experienced something that expanded my humanity: the overwhelming generosity of strangers. For the first time in my life, life seemed entirely worth living.

in my little turret, even though it was drafty and uninsulated and the condensation on the windows ran down in rivulets when I cooked. To help keep me warm, I had lots of people over for dinner. I even managed to turn out some plausible food. I remember steaming open mussels in a battered tinny saucepan, making sole véronique (with peeled grapes!), and even managing to bake an apple tart in that broiler. When I remind people that they can cook no matter where they are, I know what I'm talking about.

Of course, London was also the home of my idol Elizabeth David. At the time, she was still running her cooking equipment store, and more than once I went there with the intention of daring to introduce myself. I never worked up the courage. Instead, I lurked in the aisle, trying to catch a glimpse of her and chewing my nails. But I had her books to read; and I have them still, Penguin paperbacks with torn and dog-eared pages and my pencilled exclamation points in the margins.

After my year in London, I took off with my friend Judy Johnson on a long winding journey across Europe and into Turkey, driving a beat-up old red Austin Mini and staying at campgrounds. These travels were another awakening,

this time to the meaning of hospitality: more precisely, the no-questions-asked, totally accepting and generous sharing that seems to come so naturally from people who live close to the land. Once, while camping in the countryside near some goatherds, we woke up in the morning in our little tent, and found that they had slipped a bowl of goat's milk under our tent flap while we slept. They simply shared the best they had. I didn't know then, of course, the degree to which these experiences with food and hospitality would shape my destiny.

From Turkey, we went to Corfu, where I lived for a while on practically nothing, very simply, watching the sun and the moon rising and setting over the harbor full of colored boats and the hill covered with whitewashed houses. We swam in the ocean at dawn, and ate fish fresh out of that sunstruck sea, and we picked fruit ripened under the deep cerulean sky. For the first time in my life, I was unmistakably part of the natural rhythm of a place, and life itself seemed entirely worth living. I was beginning to understand my place in the world. I returned to Berkeley and became a Montessori teacher, but just two years later, some friends and I opened Chez Panisse.

Alice (*far right*) with schoolchildren in a village in Anatolia, Turkey, summer 1969.

look
listen
touch
smell
taste

I was at the Berkeley
Montessori School
for two years. I loved
teaching Maria
Montessori's ideas
about nourishing the
whole child and
encouraging children
to learn by doing
things themselves, by
touching and tasting
and smelling in an
ongoing education
of the senses.

23

gathering recipes from friends

MY COLUMN FOR THE *SAN FRANCISCO EXPRESS TIMES*

Before Chez Panisse opened, it often seemed like I already had a restaurant in my house. Friends were always coming over for dinner. I was living with David Lance Goines, the artist whose posters came to define the style of Chez Panisse. I had been cooking my way through Elizabeth David's books, and I started collecting all kinds of other recipes from all kinds of people—from David's mother, from Gene Opton, from my friend Martine Labro, from the neighbor across the street; then David would calligraph them, decide on an illustration, and make a linoleum block print. They were published as a recurring column in the *San Francisco Express Times,* under the heading "Alice's Restaurant" (and later published in a portfolio by David)—without, I'm sorry to say, giving proper credit to the people who shared their recipes. Looking back, I'm a little ashamed of my naïveté, too. For years, I was convinced that the only sure-fire way to make mayonnaise was to whisk in the oil with a fork on which was impaled a raw potato.

ABOVE: Alice, circa 1968. OPPOSITE: *Thirty Recipes Suitable for Framing,* by Alice Waters and David Lance Goines, 1970.

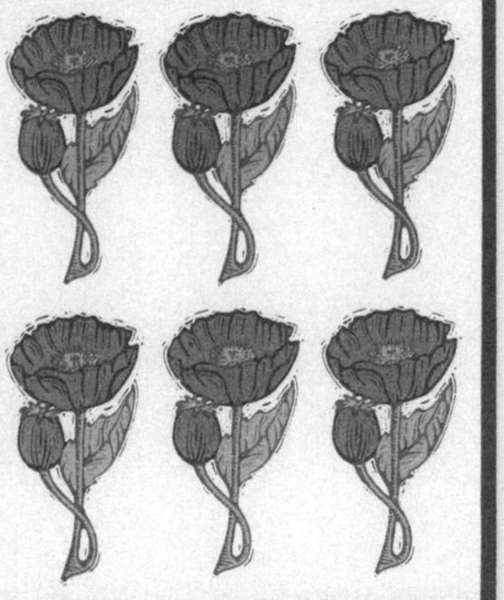

POPPYSEED STUFFING

for lamb ≈ using a mortar & pestle, mash 3 cloves of garlic & 1½ teaspoons of salt · add the following spices to the garlic mixture, mixing well with the pestle: 1 teaspoon peppercorns · ½ teaspoon curry · ⅛ teaspoon cayenne red pepper · 1 teaspoon coriander · ¼ teaspoon mace · 2 teaspoons rosemary · 2 teaspoons thyme · next · add 2 or more tablespoons of poppy seeds & 1 teaspoon of olive oil · finally, use 1 tablespoon or more of white wine to give the stuffing paste the proper consistency · either remove the bone & fill the cavity of the lamb with the stuffing · or loosen the bone & stuff around it · cover the exterior with the paste, and bake uncovered in a moderate oven · serve with yoghourt and a rice dish ·

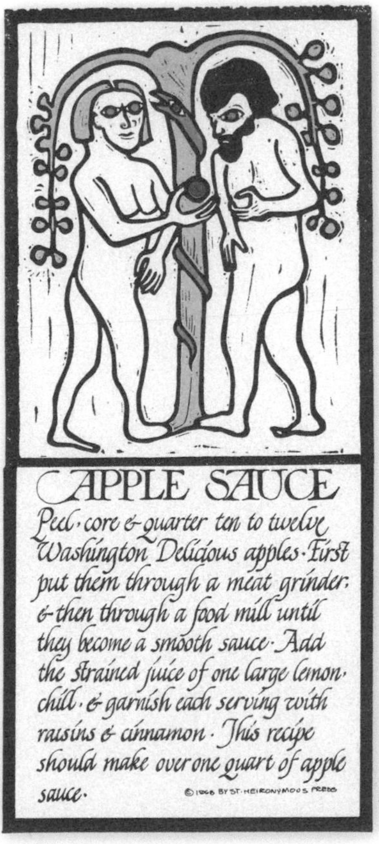

APPLE SAUCE

Peel, core & quarter ten to twelve Washington Delicious apples · First put them through a meat grinder, & then through a food mill until they become a smooth sauce · Add the strained juice of one large lemon, chill, & garnish each serving with raisins & cinnamon · This recipe should make over one quart of apple sauce ·

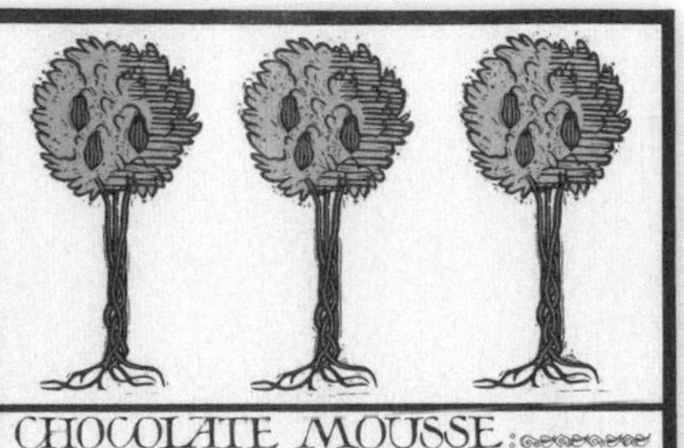

CHOCOLATE MOUSSE:

1° combine four squares of semi-sweet chocolate – 1 square equals an ounce – & two tablespoons of water in a heavy pan over a low flame, stirring occasionally. 2° when the chocolate is melted, remove from the heat & gradually stir in three egg yolks, one at a time · next, add one cube of butter, which has previously been cut into small pieces, to the chocolate mixture · 3° be sure that the mixture is very smooth before adding three stiffly-beaten egg whites · 4° put the mousse into a well-buttered mold or individual glasses, & chill · serve with melted vanilla ice cream or cream ·

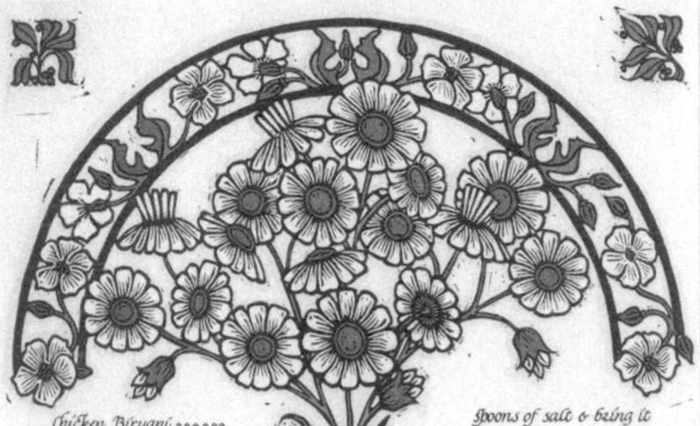

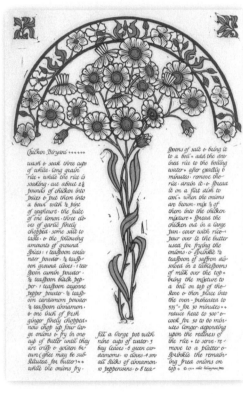

Chicken Biryani

wash & soak three cups of white, long grain rice · while the rice is soaking, cut about 2½ pounds of chicken into pieces & put them into a bowl with ½ pint of yoghourt · the juice of one lemon · three cloves of garlic finely chopped · some salt to taste, & the following amounts of ground spices: 1 teaspoon coriander powder · ½ teaspoon ground cloves · 1 teaspoon cumin powder · ½ teaspoon black pepper · 1 teaspoon cayenne pepper powder · ½ teaspoon cardamom powder · ½ teaspoon cinnamon · & one inch of fresh ginger finely chopped · now chop up four large onions & fry in one cup of butter until they are crisp & golden brown (ghee may be substituted for butter) · while the onions fry · fill a large pot with nine cups of water · 5 bay leaves · 6 green cardamoms · 10 cloves · 4 small sticks of cinnamon · 10 peppercorns · & 8 teaspoons of salt & bring it to a boil · add the drained rice to the boiling water · after exactly 6 minutes, remove the rice · drain it · & spread it on a flat dish to cool · when the onions are brown, mix ⅓ of them into the chicken mixture · spread the chicken out in a large pan · cover with rice · pour over it the butter used for frying the onions · & sprinkle ½ teaspoon of saffron dissolved in 2 tablespoons of milk over the top · bring the mixture to a boil on top of the stove & then place into the oven – preheated to 375° – for 30 minutes · reduce heat to 300° & cook for 50 to 60 minutes longer, depending upon the readiness of the rice · to serve, remove to a platter & sprinkle the remaining fried onions on top ·

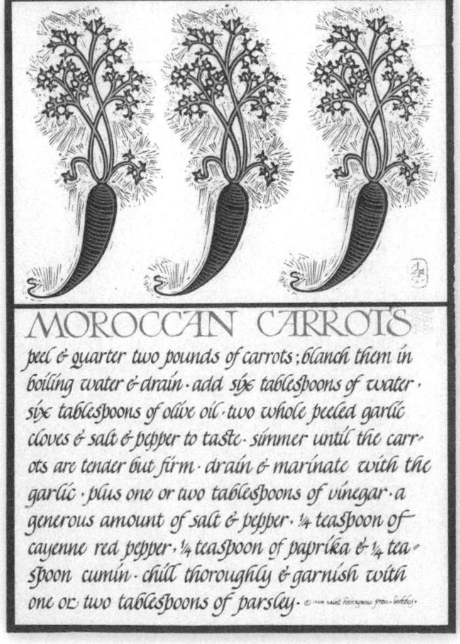

MOROCCAN CARROTS

peel & quarter two pounds of carrots; blanch them in boiling water & drain · add six tablespoons of water · six tablespoons of olive oil · two whole peeled garlic cloves & salt & pepper to taste · simmer until the carrots are tender but firm · drain & marinate with the garlic · plus one or two tablespoons of vinegar · a generous amount of salt & pepper · ¼ teaspoon of cayenne red pepper · ¼ teaspoon of paprika & ¼ teaspoon cumin · chill thoroughly & garnish with one or two tablespoons of parsley ·

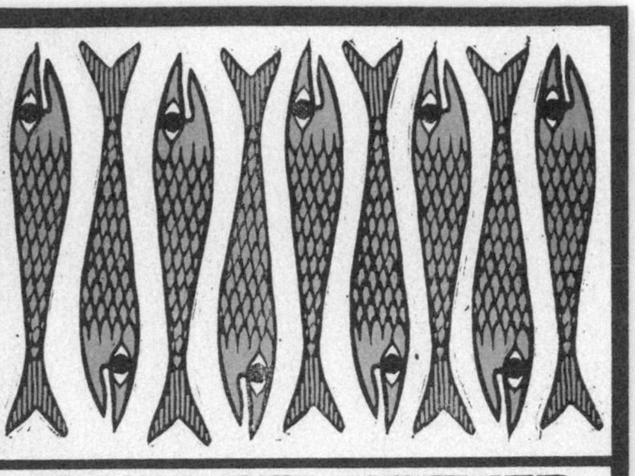

ANCHOVY STUFFED EGGS

Hard boil twelve eggs & let them cool · Cut the eggs into crosswise halves & cut a thin slice off each end so they will stand upright; reserve the end slices for later use · Remove the yolks and put them through a seive · Mix the yolks with one stick of softened butter & ⅓ cup of mayonnaise · Mash ten drained anchovy fillets & blend them with the egg yolk mixture · Now dice the reserved slices of egg white & add them to the mixture, & stir well · Season to taste with finely chopped parsley, chervil, tarragon, chopped fresh chives & pepper · Fill the egg whites with the yolk mixture using a pastry bag or a spoon · Set them on a bed of watercress ·

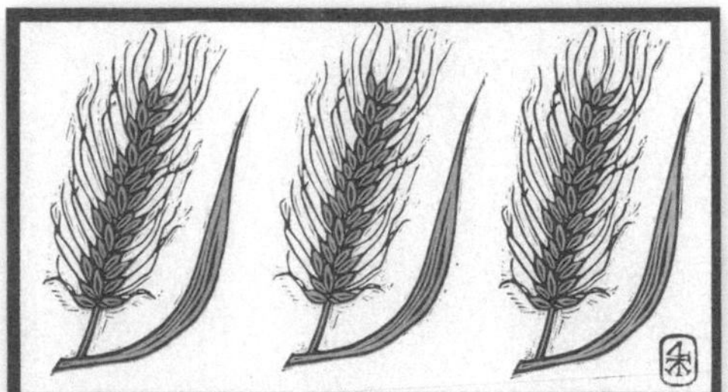

RYE BREAD

sift three cups of white flour & one cup of rye flour into a medium size bowl · add one tablespoon of cocoa · one tablespoon of caraway seed · ½ teaspoon of salt · & four tablespoons of sugar · stir in one package of dry yeast dissolved in ½ cup warm water · one egg <room temperature> & up to one cup of warm water · Mix the ingredients well: the mixture should now be of a sticky consistency · and hard to stir · knead the mixture with a wooden spoon for a few minutes & then put it in a 5"×9"×3" well greased loaf pan to rise in a warm place for 45 minutes · bake at 425° for one hour · brush the top with milk halfway through baking · after baking remove from the pan immediately & cool · any combination of flours will work well · with or without caraway seeds & cocoa ·

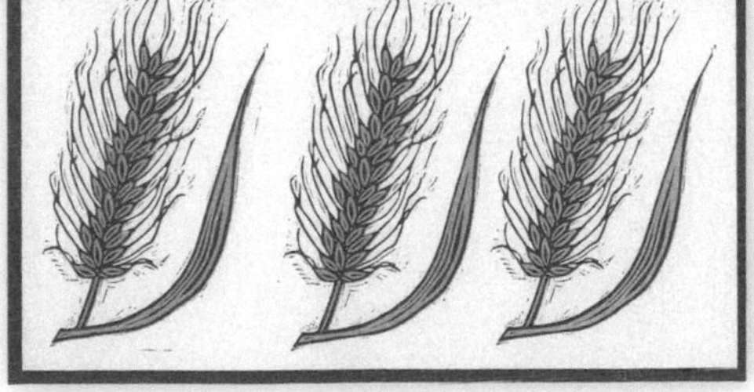

a fantasy becomes a reality

A RESTAURANT TAKES SHAPE

TOM LUDDY (*film producer and cofounder of the Telluride Film Festival*): Alice's friend Martine Labro kept telling me about Alice. I think she wanted to fix us up: Martine was that kind of lady. And Alice and I clicked. Alice was a Montessori teacher, and after school we would go to the theaters I was running and see movies, and later we would show movies at home on a 16 mm projector and Alice would cook. We would have friends over, and get some free wine from our friend who worked for Robert Mondavi. We drank those early Mondavi vintages like water. And Alice had a fantasy of opening a restaurant. I encouraged that fantasy,

because we didn't have too many good restaurants to go to at all in those days.

We had lots of fun with Martine and her husband, Claude. (When Claude and Martine's daughter, Camille, was born, we were her godparents.) We would go to Sonoma and Bolinas with them and bring along a projector. I was friends with all these poets who had moved there in the sixties, and we'd pick blackberries together and show films. There was a restaurant in Bolinas in an old Victorian house, called The Gibson House, that we really liked. They always had beautiful fresh flowers from their gardens, and they had mismatched

silverware that was obviously from flea markets. The food was OK, but the feeling of it—the vibes and the garden—was what inspired us.

We saw tons of movies at our place and at the Telegraph Repertory Cinema. I was working with Mel Novikoff, who had this wonderful, legendary theater called The Surf, in San Francisco, and it must have been there that we saw all the Marcel Pagnol movies, including the trilogy called *Marius, Fanny,* and *César.* And Alice cried and cried and cried. She saw everything she believed in in those movies. All her values were there. And she liked the restaurants in Pagnol's movies, places

I loved getting people together around the table and Tom loved getting them together in front of a movie screen. Our life together completely revolved around sharing meals and movies. Over the decades, Chez Panisse and the Pacific Film Archive grew up together in an intense, symbiotic relationship. All these years later, we're still engaged in this important collaboration between the worlds of food and film. Tom has had an extraordinarily catalytic influence on Chez Panisse.

a world of dreams, an escape, and an education

in Provence where it wasn't like the fancy restaurants in Paris, where you were intimidated if you couldn't pronounce something on the menu. And because that spirit was in Pagnol, I said, let's name it after your favorite character, Panisse, the one who really made you cry. Because she was so moved by Panisse—his sacrifice, and his selfless love. She cried about his generosity and how he knew he would lose the girl to the other guy, the younger boy. It broke her heart. And I liked the sound of it. It sounded like *fougasse*, and all those other Provençal words. And it seemed like all French restaurants were named Chez Somebody. That was the French way.

Fortunately, I had a friend, Paul Aratow, who played a critical role. Paul was somebody we knew who actually owned a house. He loved cooking and having people eating and drinking in his house.

He had the same spirit Alice had about bringing people together. Alice was very impressed that he made his spaghetti from scratch. He had copper pots and all the kitchen equipment that Alice could ever want. He was one of our few friends who wasn't either a revolutionary, a radical, a lunatic, or impoverished.

I said, Alice, let's see if we can interest Paul in this idea. And Paul was the kind of person who said, "But of course! But of course!" To him it was like a snap of the fingers. And we needed that, because Alice was insecure and nervous about whether she could do this. Paul had this very naïve but very positive attitude that "it's going to be easy, nothing could be easier! You will have fun, and it will just be like a big version of what we're doing."

I knew one other person who was young and owned a house, and that was Greil Marcus. I fig-

ured, if Greil owns a house in North Berkeley, he must have a little bit of money, too, and he likes us. So he invested a little bit. And Martine was a big influence. Martine's cooking and style—that was a picture of her on the first poster David Goines made for the restaurant. Martine and Claude were the Pagnol characters in our life.

Paul had his role. He helped find the building and remodel it. And he was confident, and in those sexist times, he projected to certain people—purveyors and contractors—that he was the kind of man who was in charge and knew how to do things. He cooked in the restaurant sometimes, too. But he left before long, when he saw there were too many people who didn't know what they were doing and that the restaurant was losing money hand over fist, and that it wasn't going to be all fun.

A group of film lovers at an early Telluride Film Festival in the seventies (*from left*): Barbet Schroeder, Manny Farber, Tom Luddy, Ed Lachman, Patricia Patterson, Werner Herzog, Jean-Pierre Gorin, and Brooks Riley.

I've been going to the Telluride Film Festival way up in the Colorado mountains since it started, about the same time as Chez Panisse. The festival is always filled with an eclectic group of impassioned people from all over the world who Tom celebrates and collaborates with—everyone from the great stars of Hollywood to provocative young filmmakers from China or Iran. I've met some of my dearest friends there. And I'll never forget seeing Abel Gance in 1979 walking down the main street in town, still alive at ninety, just before his legendary 1927 movie *Napoléon* was shown on three screens, with a live accompaniment.

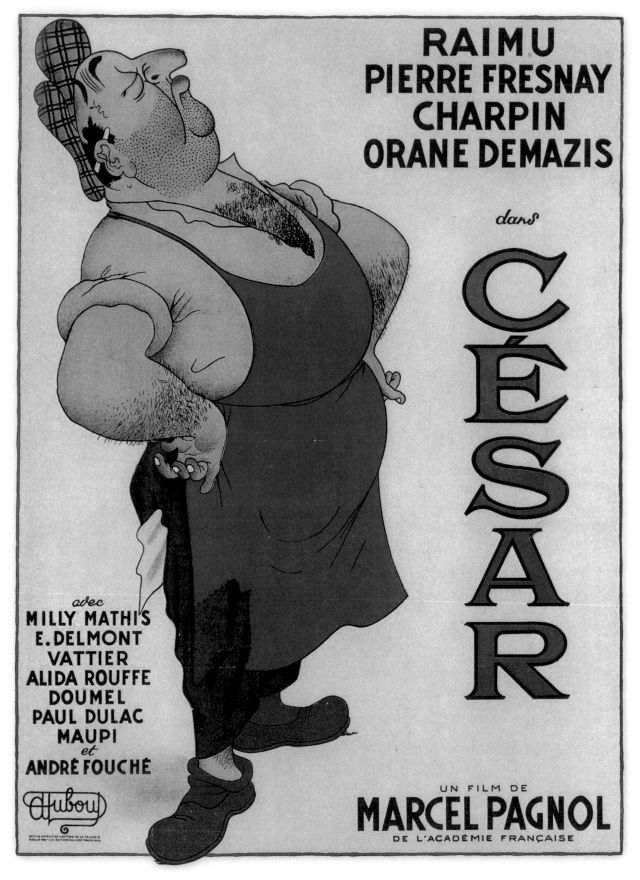

RAIMU
PIERRE FRESNAY
CHARPIN
ORANE DEMAZIS

dans

CÉSAR

avec
MILLY MATHIS
E. DELMONT
VATTIER
ALIDA ROUFFE
DOUMEL
PAUL DULAC
MAUPI
et
ANDRÉ FOUCHÉ

UN FILM DE
MARCEL PAGNOL
DE L'ACADÉMIE FRANÇAISE

Marcel Pagnol's Marseille trilogy was written for the stage, but with the advent of sound movies all three plays were filmed. The first, *Marius*, was directed by Alexander Korda in 1931; the second, *Fanny*, was directed by Marc Allégret in 1932, and the third, *César*, by Pagnol himself in 1936. These posters were designed by Albert Dubout for the films' reissue in 1950 and hang today on the walls of the Chez Panisse Café.

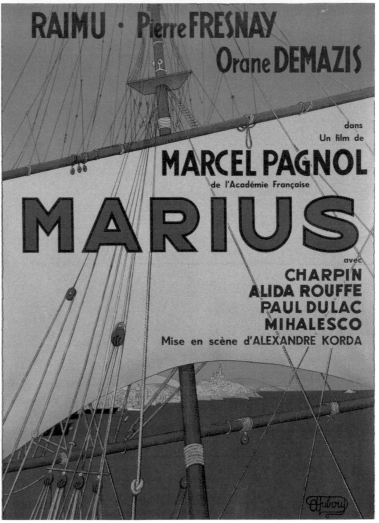

Posters by Albert Dubout for Marcel Pagnol's Marseille trilogy.

Marcel Pagnol and company

My partners and I decided to name our new restaurant after the widower Panisse, the compassionate marine outfitter who marries the pregnant Fanny after her boyfriend Marius runs off to sea. We were trying to evoke the sunny good feelings of a world that contained so much that was missing from our own—the simple good food of Provence, the atmosphere of tolerant camaraderie and great lifelong friendships, and a respect for both the old folks and their pleasures and the young and their passions. Four years later, when our partnership incorporated itself, we immodestly took the name Pagnol et Cie., Inc., to reaffirm our desire of emulating Pagnol and his actors. We were seeking to re-create an ideal reality where life was lived close to the land, where food was produced by people who were sustained by each other and by the earth itself, where life and work were inseparable, and where the daily pace left time for an afternoon anisette or a restorative game of *pétanque*.

1971
Chez Panisse opens

This is me in front of the restaurant on the day it opened. I'm wearing a polka-dot rayon dress I got from a vintage clothes store called the Bizarre Bazaar. I have no idea what I was feeling except an urgency to make things right for the opening. Our opening night menu was pâté en croûte, duck with olives, and a plum tart. The first customers wandered in while I was still nailing down the threadbare Persian runner on the stairs.

DAVID LANCE GOINES *(artist, writer)*: There was no sign to inform the passersby of the new restaurant, which still resembled nothing so much as an ordinary house. So I took thick sticks of chalk and lettered "Chez Panisse Café & Restaurant" on the wooden fence out front

Meant to be temporary, the sidewalk-chalk sign lasted until the rains began, by which time I had carved a redwood sign and painted the incised letters rose red outlined in pale gray. The sign silvered, then faded, was repainted, then faded once again and split. So I replaced it with a new curved, carved sign that has so far withstood the ravages of time.

Forty years is a long time for an outdoor sign to last. Forty years is a long time for anything to last, especially a restaurant. Chalk it up to experience.

Red-and-white-checked oilcloth tablecloths, mismatched silverware and chairs

that we found at the flea market, art deco light fixtures, bouquets of fresh flowers . . .

RAIMU · Pierre FRESNAY · CHARPIN
Orane DEMAZIS
dans

Un film de
MARCEL
PAGNOL
de l'Académie Française

CÉSAR

avec
MILLY MATHIS · E. DELMONT · VATTIER · ALIDA ROUFFE
DOUMEL · PAUL DULAC · MAUPI · ANDRÉ FOUCHÉ

IMP. MONÉGASQUE · MONTE-CARLO

a different menu every day

FOLLOWING OUR INSTINCTS

On the right, an early conversation about food at the restaurant: I'm on the left, Victoria Kroyer (*right*), and Lindsey Shere (*center*), the pastry chef, holding a copy of *The French Menu Cookbook*, by Richard Olney, one of the biggest influences on our menu planning. For dinner we had decided to serve a single new and different fixed-price menu each night, with no choices, so that we could compose a meal that was a balanced whole. We were experimenting on the public, cooking lots of things none of us had ever made before.

GREIL MARCUS *(music critic, historian, and director, Pagnol et Cie., Inc.)*: Over the next weeks and months, the gathering place Alice had imagined Chez Panisse might become began to emerge. It happened in fits and starts. "It wasn't until the next week that the food really took hold," says a woman who had shopped with Alice for dishware the week before the restaurant opened. At the very start, cooks and partners came and went quickly, but the chefs, Victoria Kroyer and Barbara Rosenblum, and Lindsey Shere, were finding their footing, and also finding their way into the restaurant as Alice imagined it: that every dish was to be made to bring out the essence of what it was, that each serving of fish, or chicken,

or asparagus, or nectarines be a thing in itself, made to orchestrate, to dramatize, what it was—made to give up its secret, that secret flavor, smell, texture, and even aura.

CHARLES SHERE *(writer, composer, and director, Pagnol et Cie., Inc.)*: The restaurant opened with women in the kitchen: Alice, Lindsey, Victoria, Leslie Land. More women followed: Joyce Goldstein, Peggy Smith, Judy Rodgers, Catherine Brandel, Eve Felder, Shelley Handler, Carolyn Dille. I've always thought the basic goodness of Chez Panisse owed a lot to the presence of these women, whose passion was for basic values and community.

Near right, an early menu designed by David Goines; far right, the menu cover it was meant to slip into. This menu was actually never used. It was instantly obsolete because it combined three meals on one page, included dishes we weren't even planning to cook every day, and didn't leave enough room to list the actual courses we did prepare for the changing fixed-price dinner. So I started writing each night's menu by hand, in the best calligraphy I could manage, and photocopying it. On the opposite page is a photo of me as a waitress, my primary role in those early days. Although we were open for breakfast it never got busy until lunch. Then it would clear out again, except for a few graduate students who would order a single espresso and spend the afternoon studying. Two of them became lifelong friends: Niloufer Ichaporia King and John Meis, who now lives in Italy, where he has helped us make invaluable culinary and cultural connections.

I loved being a waitress. I was good at persuading people who balked at being offered no choices that they were going to love what we were serving.

:CHEZ:PANISSE:
:CAFE:&:RESTAURANT:
:1517:SHATTUCK:BERKELEY:94709:
:548·5525:
:CAFE:UPSTAIRS:APERITIFS:WINE:BEER:GUINNESS:ESPRESSO:
:DESSERTS:PASTRIES:SUNDAES:

On the left is David Goines's first Panisse poster, which was on our matchboxes for over fifteen years—until we made the restaurant nonsmoking. It's a portrait of Martine Labro, a fine artist herself. Martine designed the very first poster for the restaurant—a beautiful one-of-a-kind image that we hung out front the day we opened. It was stolen that night. Opposite is a poster that David made, unsolicited, for the original Peet's Coffee & Tea store around the corner from Chez Panisse. This was a few years after we opened, and we had given up serving breakfast. Mr. Peet turned down the poster, so David offered it to us, and I immediately decided that we should start serving breakfast again. Our big breakfast was on Sunday, when Tom Guernsey made perfect *omelettes aux fines herbes* on a little portable burner. We eventually closed again because Tom got tired of working late on Saturday night and coming back early the next morning. That very same week, we were featured in a local magazine as having the best brunch in the Bay Area. We forgot to put up a now-closed-for-breakfast sign, and that Sunday people patiently lined up at the gate and around the block, all in vain.

collaborating with friends
CREATING A PARTNERSHIP

CHARLES SHERE *(writer, composer, and director, Pagnol et Cie., Inc.)*: A few of Alice's friends had lent a few dollars to open the restaurant, and she decided that they should share ownership with the key staff: Alice, Jeremiah Tower, and Lindsey in the kitchen; Jerry Budrick and Tom Guernsey on the floor; and Mary Borrelli, who was the office manager. And she flat out gave these people as big a percentage of the restaurant as she kept. Now a lot of people would think that that was a damn fool thing to do, as far as business was concerned. But in fact it was an incredibly important thing to do because that was what energized the restaurant, almost from the beginning.

It wasn't a partnership, it wasn't a corporation, it was really a community—a real community of interest where everyone was there for exactly the same reasons, and in it to exactly the same depth. I don't know of any other business that got started that way. At first it ran like a family, everyone knowing what needed to be done and doing it almost without direction. Then it grew and grew, to over a hundred employees. But it's still a family, and everyone is still passionate about the central issues: finding the best material, treating it simply and skillfully, learning from others but remembering the past. Busboys become waiters, then hosts; cooking assistants become sous-chefs, then chefs. Departments—kitchen, café, pastry, floor staff—know what their roles are, what their responsibilities are. Everyone has his own ideas, but Alice somehow integrates the group effort.

It seems fluent and intuitive, but that's deceptive: now and then the road's a little bumpy, and an outside eye is helpful to see past an immediate issue, to keep the core values alive—family, human values, sustainability, nurture. Some of us have been on the board of directors from the beginning, and that's helped keep the sense of the sixties alive into the new century.

To the left is a picture of me with Jerry Budrick (*center*) and Tom Guernsey, the two waiters who became partners. On the facing page is Tom with busboy Steve Sullivan, who later became our baker. When I was working in the restaurant all day and night, I wanted to work with people I could share something with. Not just somebody who can do the job, but somebody I liked. When you work with friends though, you run the risk that they won't always do what needs to be done and you have to tell them and sometimes it works out and sometimes it doesn't. At Chez Panisse, it mostly worked out.

artists in the kitchen

Architect Jeremiah Tower (*right*) and painter Willy Bishop (*left*) mastered another kind of art.

Under Jeremiah's incandescent leadership, the kitchen was bursting with boldness and nerve, as he aspired to new heights of gastronomic glory. We were flying by the seat of our pants—and every day we never knew quite what would happen.

GREIL MARCUS (*music critic, historian, and director, Pagnol et Cie., Inc.*): The freshness of the ingredients, the sparkle of flavors in the mouth, the way a plate could be so visually balanced and yet seem uncomposed—each of these elements was, night by night, a surprise in and of itself, so that neither the customers in the dining room nor the cooks behind the kitchen took anything for granted.

In 1973 Jeremiah Tower became the chef. He was a glamorous, charismatic person, ambitious, full of ideas, eager to try anything, heedless of obstacles. The cooking became more glamorous, too—and more baroque, elaborate, rich, in a word, luxe. Reviews began to come in, in national publications, and the clientele began to change: people from out of town, people who had heard it was the place to go but didn't know why and didn't understand why they couldn't have whatever they wanted, and what do you mean there's no bar, just wine and beer? I don't eat rabbit. I don't eat squid. Beets give me hives. What kind of place is this? The price of dinner, under four dollars at the start, rose to over ten by 1976.

emulating the past

We were reading books about Auguste Escoffier and César Ritz and places like La Pyramide and La Coupole that had history and exuberance and sophistication. We were trying to find our way to somehow re-create this time of restaurant grandeur. We were trying to live a fantasy. But the truth is, we were losing our balance a bit. . . .

ABOVE: Jeremiah in the kitchen, about 1975. **LEFT:** Ruth Reichl and her then husband, Doug Hollis. Ruth was working at The Swallow, a countercultural restaurant collective in Berkeley. **OPPOSITE:** Alice in the restaurant, circa 1974.

RUTH REICHL (*food writer*): In my very first memory of Chez Panisse, I am sitting at an upstairs table watching a tall and insanely beautiful woman standing before a heap of garlic. As we drink chilled rosé and nibble on anchovies, sliced tomatoes, and cheese we watch the pile dwindle as she methodically cuts the heart out of each clove.

How did we get there? I don't remember. I think it had been a hard night at The Swallow, and someone had suggested we stop in for a drink. What I do remember is asking the beautiful woman what she was doing, and the look she sent my way.

Slowly, she pushed her long hair out of her eyes. Then she said, "Garlic gets bitter when it starts to sprout." I felt like a squashed turnip; we'd certainly never done such a thing at The Swallow. But that was the difference between Chez Panisse and the rest of us: they were all so much more glamorous, exotic, and interesting. And, of course, they cooked better than we did.

I never walked into Chez Panisse without feeling like an Earth Shoe in a room full of Manolo Blahniks. But I kept turning up, because I always felt different by the time I left. Some time during the course of the meal a seismic shift always occurred. Looking at this picture I remember how it felt to be waiting for that moment. Dazzled by the flowers and intoxicated by the food, every sense would suddenly wake up. Then I'd relax into the experience, feeling as if this was the one place on earth where I was meant to be. When the meal was over I'd float out the door, happy to be alive, happy to be me—and very happy to be living in Berkeley.

taste
and taste
again

When cooks first come into the kitchen we learned to ask them, "What do you like to eat? What did you grow up eating? What do you cook for your friends?" The most important thing we learned to do was taste. Another spoonful, another taste. Is it all right? What does it need? And even after somebody says, "Ooh! It's just right!" you have to retaste it.

ANNE ISAAK *(restaurateur)*: I first heard of Chez Panisse in the fall of 1974. I had been cooking in San Francisco and was casting about for a restaurant that reflected my idealized food dreams. My sister Natalie suggested Chez Panisse, saying, "Annie, I think this is you." We met there for lunch and, aside from a vague impression of the entry with its welcoming sign and amazing tree, my only memory of our lunch is *oeufs durs au mayonnaise*. Two of my favorite foods on the same plate: eggs and homemade mayonnaise. It couldn't have been simpler or more appealing.

ABOVE: Alice and Willy Bishop. OPPOSITE, FROM TOP: Alice makes David Goines taste an oyster. Ann Isaak in the kitchen, about 1974.

Several days later I returned to the kitchen, empty except for a woman about my age, who was bent over the deep sink pulling out trout and slitting and cleaning them. This introduction to Alice was the beginning of more than two intense years of cooking in that kitchen and an intense lifelong attachment to the restaurant and the community that grew up around it. Before I had felt like an outsider, a young person with romantic ideas about food and culture who had chosen the blue-collar job of restaurant work, which had no cachet in America in those days. Paul Bocuse hadn't yet appeared on the cover of *Time* magazine. I was lucky enough to be hired several weeks later after an evening try-out. I've always thought the clincher was my parsley chopping skills, which I owed to the Cantonese prep cooks I had worked with at my last job.

I have so many memories of my early impressions of the restaurant: the steadying presence of Lindsey, drinking Normandy cider, dancing tangos, slurping acacia blossom-scented crème anglaise behind the closed door of the walk-in refrigerator. And so many food firsts: chervil, morel mushroom tarts, duck that wasn't *à l'orange*, all those live crayfish, Madeira cream sauce, Meyer lemons, Mexican lobsters with anchovy butter. And the creative verve of working alternately with Alice, with her great ideas and confidence, and her panic, but always squeaking through—and Jeremiah, with the tyranny of his charm and his mercurial emotional presence.

"I'm quite convinced that cooking is the only alternative to filmmaking. Maybe there is also another alternative: that's walking on foot." Werner Herzog

The director Werner Herzog had sworn he would eat his shoe if Errol Morris ever finished his first documentary, *Gates of Heaven*. When Errol's movie premiered, Werner, being a man of his word, made good on his promise. Chez Panisse helped cook the shoes (the desert boots he was wearing when he made his oath) stuffed with garlic and seethed in duck fat, and Berkeley filmmaker Les Blank (*above, at left*) recorded it all in a twenty-minute documentary called *Werner Herzog Eats His Shoe* (1979).

Werner Herzog Eats his Shoe

ABOVE: The poster for Les Blank's documentary. CLOCKWISE, FROM FAR LEFT: Werner chews on his shoe; the classic shoe-eating scene from Charlie Chaplin's *The Gold Rush* (1925); Werner shares the stage with Tom Luddy, then the director of the Pacific Film Archive, at the premier of *Gates of Heaven*. OPPOSITE: Werner's shoes before and after.

BOB WAKS (nurse): I met Alice after I started working at the Cheese Board around 1969. She adored *le fromage*; I gave her tastes. One day, after an orgy of Camembert, she offered me a job in the new restaurant. I don't remember much during the chaos of Chez's birth, but it involved food. I introduced her to Jerry Budrick, who became the flamboyantly operatic, Scrabble-playing, bowling, card-shark maître d' of the café and Alice's lover, and who fainted one night into my arms after he perforated his hand with an oyster knife. I also snagged Sharon Jones, waitress, who lived in a dollhouse in back of our communal home in Oakland. Eventually I ended up working with Willy Bishop as one of the sous-chefs. I also held the exalted position of late-night chef, serving a limited menu of steak and shoestring fries. Most of my meals ended up in staff bellies after late-night consumption of copious quantities of vino. After five years I retired, but I remain hooked to Chez and still administer annual infusions of my New Year's Eve tripe to the staff. Jean-Pierre and I share the same birthday. Amazing, no?

SHARON JONES (teacher): I had just arrived on the West Coast by way of Afghanistan, India, and Nepal, and quickly became entrenched in early-seventies Berkeley life. I was living in a commune, meditating, and buying zany secondhand clothes at Bizarre Bazaar. A few days before Chez Panisse was to open, Alice asked me to help out: "At least for the first week—we need someone to wait on tables." The moment I walked in I fell in love. The restaurant was uncommonly alive, with soft light playing on the flowers, heels clicking on the bare wood floor, and the merry-go-round of swinging kitchen doors. The smells got me the most—smashed garlic in the dressing, caramelizing duck juices, glistening fruit tarts. Who could resist? Alice seemed to be everywhere, moving quickly but not missing a thing, coaxing people and plates to the right point. That first night I knew something important was in the works here, but not how much I would be transformed by it—as would my future sons, Nico and Oliver, and so many more of us over the next forty years.

la vraie chose

One afternoon a Frenchman who had grown up hunting and cooking showed up at the kitchen door, looking for a job. He had more professional training and experience in classic French cooking than all of the rest of us put together. Whether he was roasting suckling pigs or shelling peas, Jean-Pierre Moullé brought a new sense of professionalism and gastronomic precision to our kitchen. He has stayed on for nearly thirty years.

serving it forth

When Mark Miller started cooking he brought a world of new tastes and kinds of spiciness. We began to grill more, improvising fire pits in the backyard. Mark had been a graduate student in anthropology and knew a lot about non-European cuisines. It was Mark who introduced us to the books of Diana Kennedy, the brilliant chronicler of Mexican cooking, who became a great inspiration and a true friend.

MARK MILLER *(restaurateur and food consultant)*: I've always been captivated by the immediacy of the grilling process and the intoxicating perfume of grilled foods. Grilling was a role I relished at Chez Panisse. The menu had stretched beyond the confines of the Provençal food people had come to expect, becoming more eclectic and adventurous. Everyone in the kitchen shared a sensibility of cooking simple, honest food that evoked a sense of time and place. One New Year's Eve dinner I was encouraged to re-create one of the culinary experiences that is part of my core food personality: eating fresh lobster on the beach pulled from steaming blankets of seaweed and dipped into sweet melted butter. We successfully re-created my Atlantic lobster dreams by digging up the entire backyard. We lined fire pits with rocks, built fires, and covered them with grills, added ten bushels of fresh Maine kelp, and steamed dozens of lobsters.

CHEZ·PANISSE·FOURTH·BIRTHDAY

OLIVES·ARTICHAUTS POIVRADE & ANCHOIS /↝ BRANDADE DE MORUE /↝
AGNEAU À LA BROCHE /↝ SALADE DE PIMENTS GRILLÉS & DE POMMES D'AMOUR
AU BASILIC /↝ LES FROMAGES ↝ SABAÏOUN ↝ VIN ↝ $10⁰⁰ COMPRIS·28·AUGUST

This picture was taken in our private dining room on the second floor, our *cabinet particulier*, before we remodeled in 1980. It was a room where one could dine intimately (it could be locked from inside). It had been painstakingly papered by my father with antique wallpaper I had found at the flea market.

On holidays, for staff parties, and on other special occasions we would always go to our friend Jay Heminway's winery, Green & Red Vineyard, which overlooks the Chiles Valley in the rugged hills to the east of the Napa Valley. Jay is a sculptor, his wife, Pam, is a painter, and everything around his place was made by hand. They were living the life I fantasized about—out in nature, amongst the vines, with friends and family gathered round.

JAY HEMINWAY (artist, owner of Green & Red Vineyard): The lure of life in the country drew a bunch of us city mice away. This led very quickly to planting gardens and even vineyards. The thrill of growing flavorful food spilled over to cooking it. Friends and friends of friends spent days and months helping build and plant, and at last—a first harvest in 1976. All interspersed with long and raucous meals, and music, and a little dancing. One of those friends of a friend was Ms. Alice Waters (daughter Tobin's Montessori School teacher) always encouraging growing and always a good friend .

For years many Thanksgivings were celebrated here by this band of friends. The feast got more delicious each year with wild fowl, wild mushrooms, and wild wine. Fond memories.

A gathering of friends and family at Jay and Pam's on Thanksgiving Day, 1980.

thanksgiving

searching
for ingredients

From the very beginning of the restaurant we searched for ingredients that would make the food taste like the best things I had eaten back in France. In the early days we would find and pick things we needed from everywhere around us: wild fennel from the railroad sidings in West Berkeley, plum blossoms and acacia blossoms from the trees that lined our streets, blackberries from the brambles of Bolinas, wild watercress from streams alongside back roads in Marin County, nasturtium flowers from the gardens of our neighbors. We encouraged amateur gardeners and mycologists to share their harvests. We knocked on the doors of strangers to ask if we could pick the mulberries from their trees. I drove back and forth to the fish and poultry markets of Chinatown so often, hauling leaky boxes of rock cod and ducks, that my car began to smell so bad that nobody would ride in it.

foraging
for
taste

ALAN TANGREN *(farmer, writer, former Chez Panisse chef and forager)*: Alice had established the principle for choosing ingredients at the restaurant: use only the freshest and finest available. And the cooking style of the restaurant was evolving. Instead of following French or Mediterranean recipes we were paring ideas down to their essential core and preparing food that enhanced the essence of the ingredients and presented them in an artful way.

Chez Panisse found young tender lamb in the foothills of Amador County at the Dal Porto Ranch, brightly flavored goat cheese in Sonoma made by Laura Chenel, and ducks in the streetside markets of San Francisco's Chinatown. And the backyard gardens of a few dedicated customers would provide us with a few bunches of crisp sweet radishes. Yes, this was what we wanted, but we wanted more.

Fortunately, we were not well acquainted with the conventional wholesale meat and produce dealers with their endless stacks of cardboard boxes bursting with what most other restaurants accepted as fresh and fine. Instead, we would poke around local markets, picking through piles of green beans at the grocery store or using just the hearts of leaf lettuces. Without knowing it, we had planted the seed of "foraging."

And we knew there were people in our area who were producing the products we needed. Bill Fujimoto at Monterey Market had a knack for finding remarkable farmers; often he was able to provide a box of ripe peaches for Lindsey that had the perfect balance of sweet and tart.

Other producers began showing up at the kitchen door with a box of lettuces, maybe a little bigger than the ones we really wanted. But they were fresh and sweet and cut that morning. And maybe the berry grower on the other side of the hills could plant a few more vines if we promised a market for his fruit. But we needed a real connection to people who were growing things.

We slowly discovered that the people who were obsessive about growing the best-tasting produce were also concerned about the health of the soil, the welfare of beneficial insects and other animals, and the clarity of the water running off their fields. They were interested in rediscovering older varieties that were harder to grow, and less prolific, but much tastier, and which brought a sense of continuity with the past to both their fields and our tables.

It turned out that we wanted the products of growers who saw a larger consequence to their lives than simply growing and selling food. Many of the chefs were acquainted with one or two exceptional farmers. One day Alice and I sat down to think about how to find these exceptional farmers and bring them into the restaurant. The idea for a Chez Panisse forager began to take shape.

The "forager," a name we appropriated from its more conventional sense, would be the point person, responsible for all the food that came into Chez Panisse, and who would be, in a way, the conscience of the restaurant.

Carrie Glenn decorated the restaurant with flowers for thirty-five years. She foraged for her materials in the same way we foraged for food. In the picture above she is carrying daffodils from one of our earliest suppliers of flowers and produce, Ina Chun. Carrie was a consummate artist, and her flowers were extraordinary. She had an aesthetic that was deep and complex and inspirational. There were several people in the neighborhood who would come into the restaurant only to see the flowers and leave without ever ordering any food.

foraging for beauty

loaves and fishes

PAUL JOHNSON *(owner, Monterey Fish)*: I started delivering fish to Chez Panisse and things seemed to go well—except the menu was still only a vague guideline, the freshest fish never seemed to be the one that was on the menu that night, and I was always late, usually showing up with something other than what they were expecting. I was always impressed with how they could deal with the unpredictability of what I would bring. If the menu read rock cod and I walked in with California halibut straight off a local fisherman's boat, there was always encouragement and appreciation—never complaints. I remember one particularly trying but rewarding night when I showed up at five-fifteen (service began at six) with dripping buckets of seaweed and barnacle-encrusted wild Pacific mussels gathered at the last minute at the mouth of Tomales Bay. For a short while panic ensued—but

at the end of the night everyone raved. Another time, I remember dragging a big, rope-handled wooden box up the alley to the kitchen on a night they had put bouillabaisse on the menu. Inside the box was a mess of rockfish, still in rigor, chile pepper red, emerald green, bright orange, and on top, a few live, squirming local wolf eels. The kitchen staff, led by Jean-Pierre with cleaver in hand, didn't hesitate a second: they quickly reduced that box of fish to the best bouillabaisse I've ever tasted.

STEVE SULLIVAN *(owner, Acme Bread Company)*: When I was in London I had picked up Elizabeth David's new bread book, and I read myself to sleep with it in fields and pensions and spare rooms, as I biked around in France. I think Elizabeth David's books had made Alice want to cook dinner for people, and when I read this one, it made me want

to bake bread for people. Back in Berkeley I was soon baking bread every day in my student co-op kitchen. It started off pretty bad, but folks at the restaurant (and my roommate's mother) helped me get on track. Everyone seemed to be rooting for me to finally do something meaningful! And the bread gradually improved, and people began to welcome it, and eat it, and even keep it when I brought it around. Then Alice noticed. Or maybe she had been paying attention all along. At any rate, one afternoon she told me that the lack of good bread at the restaurant had become terribly depressing, that she wanted the Chez Panisse community to have a baker it could depend on and that she wanted bread to be at the center of things at the restaurant. And that she just sort of wondered whether there was any slight chance that I might have some inclination to bake it.

In the mid-seventies Richard Olney introduced me to the Peyraud family at their winery in Provence, the Domaine Tempier, outside the little port city of Bandol. I felt like I'd walked straight into a Marcel Pagnol movie. Lucien became my surrogate father and Lulu became my muse. Their love of wine and food and the place they lived—and of each other— became the lodestar of my life.

Lucien Peyraud, patriarch of the Domaine Tempier, holds forth at table flanked by Richard Olney and my friend Nathalie Waag, circa 1980.

KERMIT LYNCH *(wine merchant, writer)*: Some may say that I "discovered" the wines of Domaine Tempier, but they would be wrong. Alice and Jeremiah had been there first and asked importer George Linton to bring some cases in for Chez Panisse before I had an import house. I received my first shipment after that, which included the 1971 Cuvée Spéciale (four years in *foudre* before it was finished and bottled). When it reached Berkeley, I traded nine cases of it (somber and thick) for the 1972 (bright and fruity), which was already on the Chez Panisse wine list.

Alice and I both found our way to Tempier through Richard Olney, who introduced me to the domaine. In the years to follow, we both visited so often and were received so well, we felt like part of the family. We wined and dined into the wee hours—Lulu's celebrated home cooking, Lucien's bold cuvées. . . . His wines were never too old or too young to drink down, and did we ever! No one could outgenerous Lulu and Lucien.

Could it have been Alice and Richard Olney dancing in the cellar of *foudres* to Edith Piaf or Django Reinhardt, or have I heard about it so often from Lulu that I feel as if I'd been there? During the cheese course one evening, was I literally under the table in the presence of wine critic Robert Parker and his wife? It was one divine occasion after another, a vision of how life can be lived, and many of us were marked forever by our good fortune.

And so convenient—with the Panisse kitchen and my import permit, Alice and I could remind ourselves of our home away from home, starting with a glass of Bandol rosé.

Above, the Peyraud family and friends celebrating the end of the harvest in front of the domaine. Above right (*from left*): Kermit Lynch, Stephen Singer, Lulu Peyraud, Jean-Marie Peyraud, and Valérie Peyraud. Below right, Kermit Lynch emerging from the hand-hewn cellars at Richard Olney's house in Solliès-Toucas, not far from Bandol.

joie de vivre

Lulu's kitchen: my home away from home

French Impressions

CAMILLE LABRO *(food writer):* I was born a few blocks away from Shattuck Avenue, less than a year before the restaurant opened. We moved to Provence when I was very small and I've lived in France for most of my life thereafter, yet every time I go back to Chez Panisse, it feels just like home. My mom, Martine, still talks about the long evenings they spent at the restaurant, when all their friends would gather to cook, eat, drink, and talk. Every morning, she'd push me in my vintage baby carriage through the streets of Berkeley to the restaurant, where she would have a café au lait and I would take my morning nap. Chez Panisse is in my heart.

In the summer of 1975, I took my first real vacation from the restaurant and rented a farmhouse that belonged to Nathalie Waag, a friend of Martine's and Claude's who lived in the Lubéron region of Provence. Martine and Claude had moved back to Provence, not too far away. It was a magical summer. I learned what it's like to relax with a glass of anisette in the summer evening while listening to the monotonous thrumming of the cicadas among the olive trees. Martine's daughter, Camille, was already six years old, and the night the picture on the left was taken the three of us had all dressed up in our summer party dresses for a village fête. Martine had always been a role model to me, the model of a very French kind of aesthetic discernment and practical frugality. It was Martine who taught me the importance of getting the lighting just right in a room, and how to find wonderful vintage dresses at the flea market, and how to flavor a vinaigrette with just enough garlic. Her daughter, Camille, is grown up now, with kids of her own, and she is as effortlessly elegant and stylish as her mother.

lunch with Richard Olney

A KITCHEN, A PAINTING STUDIO, AND A GARDEN IN SOLLIÈS-TOUCAS

I first met Richard Olney, the painter, food writer, cook, and authority on the food and wine of France, when he was on a book tour in California. Thanks to Tom Luddy, I helped arrange a reunion between him and the filmmaker Kenneth Anger at Chez Panisse. But I didn't really get to know Richard until August of that summer of 1975 when I went to visit him for lunch at his house in the hills above the village of Solliès-Toucas in Provence. Nathalie drove me there. It was a boiling hot day, and I was beside myself with anxiety. What should I bring? What should I wear? I remember everything about the lunch he served: there was a *salade composée* like the ones we made at Chez Panisse a million times afterward: green beans, rocket picked from his garden, hard-boiled eggs from the chickens in his chicken house, hyssop flowers, and an anchovy vinaigrette. He had beautiful goat cheeses laid out on fig leaves and a dessert of apricots and a glass of Sauternes. We talked easily and at length about—everything! His kitchen was pretty much my platonic ideal of a kitchen: a fireplace in the corner, stacks of pots, and marble mortars, shelves full of rare and old cookbooks, a little bed in the corner, and in the center of the room, a pillar plastered with memorable wine labels holding it all up. After lunch he showed us his paintings. I left in a trance, feeling like we were best friends.

roots firmly in the ground

I thought I had to bring lettuce with its roots still in the dirt so that when I got to New York it would still be alive. Jean-Pierre and I arrived the day after Easter, he with a whole spring lamb slung over his shoulder and I carrying the precious lettuces.

In 1979, with Paul Prudhomme from Louisiana, I was invited to cook at an event in New York City alongside several French chefs as a representative of the young chefs of America. I was both flattered and intimidated because it was the first time I'd been to New York as a cook and also because one of the French chefs was Alain Dutournier, a dominant figure at the time.

We wanted to bring the perfect things from the West Coast, and as usual, I talked over the menu with everyone. I talked with Darrell Corti, the well-known connoisseur, about what wine to bring. I talked to people in the restaurant about what the perfect food might be. We decided on a menu of oysters on the half shell (a little presumptuous, I know—bringing oysters to New York—but I loved the little Olympic ones that came from Puget Sound), the inevitable baked goat cheese, and since it was spring, whole heads of garlic and a whole lamb to grill.

One of the most important things to me was to bring fresh salad. At the time, we had a garden in the backyard of Duke McGillis, our restaurant doctor, whose house was nearby and who took care of us all, both medically and horticulturally. I thought at the time that in order for the salad to be at its freshest, it had to be picked right before you ate it, so I came up with this idea to bring the lettuces to New York with their roots and earth still attached. In this way, I could pick the lettuce there at Tavern on the Green, where the lunch was to be held. Jean-Pierre and I must have been quite a sight carrying flats of lettuce still in the dirt onto the plane at the Oakland airport.

We arrived in New York the day after Easter and got to Tavern on the Green around nine that night. The restaurant was in full swing—waiters picking up dishes, cooks busily clanging pots and pans, people running everywhere. I remember there was a salad spinner that looked like it was eight feet in diameter. And here were Jean-Pierre and I—Jean-Pierre with a lamb slung over his shoulder and me with these earthy flats of salad. I was afraid to put the salad in their huge walk-in because I thought it would get lost or even contaminated. Luckily, a chef there put our food in a special locker with Paul Prudhomme's ingredients.

The next night was Paul Prudhomme's dinner, and it was a revelation to me. He cooked seafood andouille and pickled okra, étouffée, and all the specialties from K-Paul's. But the pièce de résistance was the dessert—individually constructed Cajun cottages assembled out of chocolate. There was one on every plate. The roof came off, and they filled each one with the perfect strawberries they had brought up from Louisiana. I'd never had a strawberry like that. I'll never forget the taste of them. Once served, the waiters came around and poured warm crème anglaise onto the cottages and the whole thing melted on the plate. I couldn't believe it. I was impressed.

Our lunch was the next day. It was the first day of spring and everyone was outside in Central Park. We had planned to grill the lamb outside, which was something that was not done very often at the time. Looking back I can see how naïve an idea this was. What if it had rained? Jean-Pierre and I were so anxious we got to the kitchen around seven-thirty in the morning and got to work: me "picking the salad" and Jean-Pierre butchering the lamb.

Luckily for us, Paul Prudhomme wandered in to see what we were up to. "Are you here just by yourselves?" he asked. "Is there anybody helping you?"

I told him I thought everything was OK, that we'd planned a simple menu.

"I think you need help," Paul replied and almost magically summoned this brigade of seventeen people to assist us. "Three people on oysters!" he commanded. "You build the fire! Two people help with the grill!"

Everything conspired to make it a successful lunch. I remember editor Judith Jones brought Southern food expert and chef Edna Lewis down to eat. The oysters were delicious. The baked heads of garlic tasted great with the 1971 Stony Hill Chardonnay. Everyone loved the spring lamb and the Ridge Zinfandel. And the baked goat cheese on that freshly picked salad? Well, when they wrote about it in the *New York Times* the next day, all they talked about were the American cooks and not the French.

Every time I see Paul at Meals on Wheels benefits and other gatherings, I think of his generosity of spirit that day.

10

Chez Panisse

CHEZ·PANISSE
TENTH · BIRTHDAY
SUNDAY · AUGUST 30TH · 1981 · JOS · PHELPS WINERY
200 TAPLIN ROAD ‡ SAINT HELENA · CALIFORNIA
AT FOUR O'CLOCK ‡ MUSIC · FOOD & WINE ‡ $25
ADVANCE RESERVATIONS REQUIRED ‡ 548-5525

Our tenth birthday party at the Joseph Phelps Vineyard was the first time we had ever gone forth into the world beyond Berkeley and staged a big event on another site, in someone else's neighborhood. It was a challenge to try and be there without interrupting their work and getting in the way. This was the first of many events when we took Chez Panisse out on the road and had to learn how to be ourselves somewhere new, bringing out the best qualities of a place without imposing on it.

BRUCE NEYERS (owner, Neyers Vineyards): In 1981, I was working for Joseph Phelps Vineyards in the Napa Valley, and one morning Joe Phelps called me into his office to explain that he had dined at Chez Panisse the night before and suggested to Alice that the winery would be the ideal place for the party. The winery is beautiful, and the prospect of hundreds of friends of Chez Panisse gathering there for a summer celebration of food and wine was a bright one. And with any luck the date wouldn't conflict with the harvest, which normally begins a little later.

The first planning meeting was held at the winery in late June so that the key people involved could see the site firsthand. My wife, Barbara, had been a cook at Chez Panisse for a couple years, and she prepared dinner after the meeting. We all sat outside on the winery terrace, with its fabulous view of the heart of the Napa Valley, enjoying one of those early summer evenings in Northern California when the weather is perfect. With Alice, Tom Guernsey, Peggy Smith, and a dozen others, we ate Barbara's marvelous fried chicken and drank several bottles of wine from my cellar. By the end of the evening, everyone agreed the site would work.

The next two months were filled with discussions about entertainment and the guest list and the food. Alice's idea from the beginning was to celebrate the summer and the bounty of nature, and when the concept of a carnival with food booths was decided on, our plans gradually began to take shape. To accommodate musicians, we arranged for a portable stage. The headliner was to be Clifton Chenier, the King of Zydeco, and his Red Hot Louisiana Band.

The day before the party, electricians worked feverishly installing outdoor lights around the winery, bringing power out to the stage, and setting up a sound system. A mountain of chairs, tables, plates, glasses, and silverware was delivered by a local rental service. Food deliveries went on until late in the evening. In the meantime, unexpectedly, the winery had become caught up in the 1981 harvest, which had already begun. The weekend of the party proved to be the harvest's absolute peak, with almost 50 percent of the grapes that were processed that year scheduled to arrive that same weekend. It was the earliest harvest in history. No one slept.

The day of the party arrived. Many had stayed up most of the night. My house looked like an adult slumber party. I was reminded of the scene in the Woodstock documentary when Wavy Gravy announces over the PA system that breakfast in bed will be served—for 400,000. We served breakfast and began to set up the food booths. Barbara had persuaded a nearby farmer who grew corn to pick a thousand ears that morning. It was grilled and served unshucked. Joe's housekeeper, Fidelfa Cruz from Oaxaca, served tortillas with mole she made by hand with a mortar and pestle. Our local butcher, Tom Catterson, famous at the time for having the country's smallest USDA-inspected meat-packing facility, prepared hundreds of sausages, grilled them on a huge mesquite grill, and served them on rolls baked that morning in the Chez Panisse kitchen. One busy booth served just-sliced, vine-ripened, organic tomatoes, drizzled with local olive oil. Open bottles of wine and platters of raw vegetables were everywhere, and servers wandered around all day refilling glasses.

It was a great day for catching up with old friends and making new ones; there was talking, hugging, kissing, comparing photos, and every other form of conviviality. Paul Prudhomme flew in from New Orleans. Paul Draper drove up from Ridge Vineyards. Darrell Corti had a driver chauffeur him from Sacramento, and he looked especially dashing in his cape. Filmmaker Les Blank was there, and Tom Luddy, then the director of the Pacific Film Archive. Francis Ford Coppola arrived just in time for dinner. The legendary rubbed elbows with the important, and occasionally with a mere Chez Panisse loyalist.

The entertainment was brilliant. Clifton Chenier was never better. Two other local bands played, a magician wandered through the crowd doing tricks, and a juggler performed on stilts, while stills from Marcel Pagnol and Les Blank films were projected onto a sheet suspended from the trellis overhead.

When the music was finally over, and the food consumed, there was still wine to be drunk, and the party continued. By then the crowd had dwindled down to twenty or so hardy souls who, led by Bob Waks, began harmonizing on old sixties tunes. Eventually the last guest wandered off, the last car disappeared down the hill, and I looked around and saw that I was alone. It was the greatest party of my life.

high spirits in the vineyard

CLOCKWISE, FROM TOP LEFT: Eleanor Coppola; Alice and her niece, Emilie Pierce, and standing behind them *(from left)* James Moore, Alexandre Waag, Tim Piland, and Pat Edwards; Jeremiah Tower, waiting to go aloft in the tethered balloon. OPPOSITE, TOP RIGHT: Joe Phelps and Alice.

after the harvest

After just about every party at Chez Panisse, we turn up the music and dance. Lots of times we pass the hat and collect money so that we can keep the musicians going for another hour or two. This party was no exception. Looking at this picture now makes me nostalgic: to see so many people who I knew really well and who I haven't seen in a long time. On the left, smiling at her partner, is Daidie Donnelley, still a member of our board of directors after all these years.

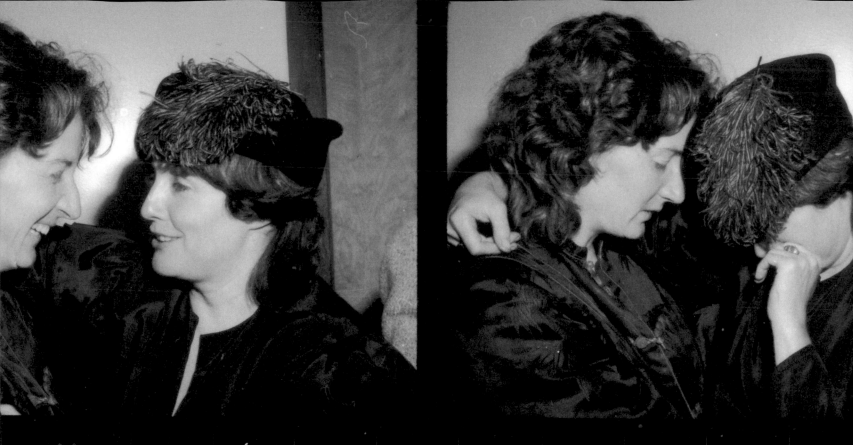

"I'M HAPPY JUST TO DANCE

Patricia Curtan
jokes with Alice.
OPPOSITE: Daidie
Donnelley dances
with Fritz Streiff.

WITH YOU." The Beatles

PATRICIA CURTAN *(artist and writer)*: When I think back to the early days of the restaurant, mostly what I recall is the vitality of the place, the energy and excitement. We were young and naïve (I wasn't yet twenty-one when I joined in) and ready to throw ourselves into something wholeheartedly. The daily momentum of the work, of making it all happen every day, was all-consuming.

I remember the anticipation of going to work on Friday and reading the menus for the forthcoming week to see what was in store—often Jean-Pierre and Alice would put dishes on the menu that we had never cooked before. We started each day in the kitchen with a cook's meeting, going over each course, exchanging ideas, deciding who would do what. It was a fast-paced collaboration and at times it felt like a high-wire act. When it all worked, when extraordinary ingredients and technique came together, it was a spectacular feeling.

There was scant division between work life and social life. We worked together into the night, and after hours we would eat and drink, and finally slow down enough to go home. On our days off we gathered at one or another's apartment and cooked for each other. Friends would arrive with a bushel of oysters, some Champagne, the makings of a pasta. We talked and talked about our little universe of food and the restaurant, and then the dancing would begin ("Bennie and the Jets"!). Eventually we wore ourselves out, and parted to retreat and rest before starting another week and doing it all again. It was enormous fun.

A few of us had just gotten back from Italy and were thinking it would be wonderful if we could have a wood-burning pizza oven. It would smell so good and be so inviting. So, we remodeled and turned the upstairs into an à la carte café that opened on April Fools' Day in 1980. Opposite, Michele Perrella throws a pizza, which he did in the Café for over two decades.

CHEZ PANISSE CAFÉ OPENS

APRIL FOOLS' DAY

GREIL MARCUS *(music critic, historian, and director, Pagnol et Cie., Inc.)*: It was determined that the restaurant would have to become two: the more expensive one-menu, fixed-price, two-seatings-a-night tablecloth place on the first floor, and an open-kitchen, no reservations, high-turnover café on the second. The idea was, too, that the restaurant would finally make money: the crowds in the Café would support the little culinary laboratory downstairs. Of course it didn't turn out that way. Prices in the Café had to be kept low, but not the cost of ingredients or what people were paid, so the Café too would barely break even, if it did.

The building was pushed back almost to the edge of the property lot; posters from the Fanny trilogy went up on the new walls. The Café opened April 1, 1980. In the Café, too, the food changed every day, just as it did downstairs, but there was a menu you could choose from—baked goat cheese with garden lettuce salad, a plate of tomatoes so full of different tastes they all but sang on the table, a carrot and coriander soup, asparagus with blood orange vinaigrette, pasta alla Norma, goat cheese and prosciutto calzone, and pizzas from a wood-burning brick oven. You could come with friends and order half the menu, crowding your table for three hours or more; you could sit down with another person, or alone, choose one or two items, and walk away forty-five minutes later, feeling as welcome or anonymous as you might in your own home, knowing that in a week or even a day you'd be back.

I was so grateful for the new life and spirit the Café brought with it, and its exuberant young staff. It changed Chez Panisse overnight. We went from about fifty employees to over a hundred and started serving more than three times as many customers, all of which brought a whole raft of new challenges. We couldn't take as many risks and whimsically do whatever we wanted anymore. There were too many livelihoods at risk if we couldn't sell all the food, so we had to be cautious with the Café menu at first. We didn't dare put rabbit on the menu, for example, and once when we had to serve grilled skewered goat's liver (left over from a downstairs dinner when we had served roast kid), we listed it on the menu as "brochette Provençale."

JACQUELINE WEST (*costume designer*): I loved the downstairs restaurant, but I didn't eat there that much. I used to go to the café upstairs before it was the Café—when it only served breakfast, and desserts and late-night things. But when the new Café opened up in 1980, as a restaurant separate from the dining room downstairs, my friends and I could finally hang out at Chez Panisse all the time. In those days I had a little clothing store right next door, so I really was there a lot. And, of course, one of the first pizza makers was my husband, Skip. Michele Perrella was the other one, and he worked there a lot longer than Skip; he became a real institution. My daughter Naomi would sit on the counter and Michele and Skip would feed her pizzas—because Skip was her dad and Michele just liked her, like he did Fanny, Alice's daughter.

When Naomi was three she went missing from the store one day. I looked everywhere. I was frantic. I went running next door to the Café to tell Skip that she was gone, and there she was, downstairs in the empty dining room, with a napkin tucked into her T-shirt, sitting with Alice. Alice was teaching her to eat oysters on the half shell and to drink the juice! Sweet, right?

Two nights in the Café I'll never forget: A party where Alice and I were dancing tangos on the tabletops and I traded my thirties silver shoes for a snood. And another, years later, when this wonderful Argentinian friend of mine, Tepa, called and asked me to go see Ástor Piazzolla at Zellerbach Hall on the campus. I said yes, but I have to bring Alice because she loves tango. The concert was so good that Alice invited the band back to the Café. They sat at that long table and Alice fed them basically everything on the menu that night. We were all sitting there and they started playing music on their water glasses. They drank the water to various levels so they could get this whole range of tones, and the whole restaurant fell silent listening to them play Ástor Piazzolla and his quintet playing this nuevo tango music with their fingers on their water glasses.

CHEZ PANISSE CAFE MENU

1517 SHATTUCK AVENUE, BERKELEY, CALIFORNIA 94709 :: 548-5049
OPEN 11:30 AM TO MIDNIGHT, MONDAY THROUGH SATURDAY
LAST SEATING AT 11:30 PM

5th BIRTHDAY
APRIL 1, 1985

SPECIAL BIRTHDAY MENU
Parsleyed ham salad
Duck two ways: braised & grilled
Artichoke and herb noodle gratin
Chino strawberry semifreddo

20.00

Garden salad 4.50
Baked goat cheese with rocket & herbs 5.50
Asparagus with blood orange vinaigrette 5.50
Duck rillettes with vegetable salads 5.50
Radicchio & roast lamb with tapenade 6.00
Endives with bagna cauda 4.50

Spring vegetable ragoût 6.00
Spring vegetable ragoût with herb pasta 8.50
Shellfish ravioli with mirepoix & saffron 9.50
Grilled lamb chops with anchovy butter
      & potato gratin 12.50

Brandade with garlic croûtons 5.50
Pizzetta with smoked salmon & salmon caviar 7.50
Miniature calzone with goat cheese & rocket 7.00
Small pizza with roasted peppers, eggplant,
      capers, anchovies & olives 8.50

Pineapple clafoutis 3.50
Chocolate truffle ice cream 3.25
Strawberries in balsamic vinegar & cookies 3.75
Rhubarb cobbler with vanilla ice cream 3.75

NV Billecart–Salmon Brut 30.00
1983 Vernaccia di San Gimignano,
      Teruzzi & Puthod 9.00
1984 Joseph Phelps Vineyards Early Harvest
      Riesling 12.00
1982 Saint Joseph, Raymond Trollat 12.00
1982 Neyers Winery Chardonnay 18.00

1983 Bandol Rosé Domaine Tempier 14.00
1982 Chianti Classico Riserva,
      Casavecchia di Nittardi 9.00
1983 Qupé Syrah 12.00
1980 Green & Red Zinfandel 12.00
1981 Bandol, Cuvée la Migona,
      Domaine Tempier 18.00

We do not accept credit cards; we do accept personal checks.
Corkage, $5.

GREIL MARCUS *(music critic, historian, and director, Pagnol et Cie., Inc.)*: The Café chefs—from Joyce Goldstein at the start to the late Catherine Brandel, Peggy Smith, David Tanis, Shelly Handler, Carolyn Dille, Gilbert Pilgram, Russell Moore, Cal Peternell, and Beth Wells—practiced a cooking that spoke the language of Alice in Wonderland. On your way to your table, you passed a vase of flowers that seemed to have grown from the table on which it stood, a counter with a platter of purple artichokes, a tart from which a slice had yet to be taken: it all said, eat me. More than that: talk to me. Ask me questions. Ask where I came from, and why I look the way I do. It was as if, with their fingers touching every ingredient, changing its shape and its form as it went from the cutting board or the oven or the stove to the plate, the cooks were speaking through the food.

PEGGY SMITH *(owner, Cowgirl Creamery)*: I started out as a cook downstairs, and a few years later I became one of the upstairs Café chefs. One of the best things about that job was that for ten years, while writing the menu every morning, I got to talk on the phone to our purveyors: Paul Johnson at Monterey Fish, Bill Fujimoto at the Monterey Market, Bob Cannard at the farm, Bud Hoffman at his chicken farm, Philip Paine at his game bird farm, to name only a few. Over the years they became the people who really drove the menu. It wasn't just about us having crazy ideas and trying to execute them anymore: the menu became more and more responsive to what our suppliers had to offer.

Over time the Café and the restaurant worked together to develop practical routines and systems that were environmentally responsible, connected us to sustainable small-scale local economies, and saved money, too. We saved our used frying fat to be recycled into biofuel; and we saved the kitchen's compostable waste and hauled it to Bob's farm when we sent the truck to pick up his vegetables. Chez Panisse was constantly evolving. And it was a good, safe place for us to push our limits: we were always applauded for exploring new areas of expertise and for mastering new techniques.

Amy Dencler (*top, at right*), started cooking in the Café and later moved to the downstairs kitchen, a cycle that has repeated itself more than a few times. Peggy Smith (*opposite*) ran the Café for many years.

upstairs downstairs

PRIX FIXE AND À LA CARTE

In the Café no less than downstairs, having food on display has always been vital to my conception of the ambiance of the place—the fruits of the season, the tart just out of the oven, the tray of candied citrus peel and little cookies—so that the customers walking by have their senses stimulated and their appetites tantalized, while being reminded of the time of year and the restaurant's capabilities. And when the customers can see the cooks it demystifies what's going on in the kitchen and invites everyone in.

fire at Chez Panisse

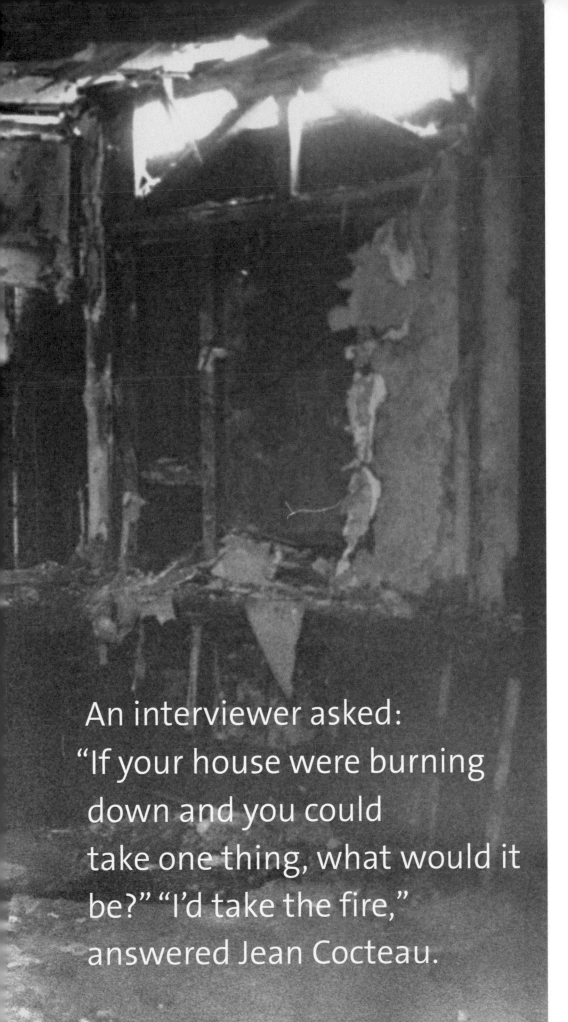

An interviewer asked: "If your house were burning down and you could take one thing, what would it be?" "I'd take the fire," answered Jean Cocteau.

My phone rang at about four o'clock in the morning on March 7, 1982: the restaurant was on fire. I was living close by, and I hurried over in time to see flames still shooting out the windows. I stood by, wringing my hands while the firefighters swarmed over the building with their ladders and hoses. They put out the fire in time to keep the second story from igniting, and they saved the building from collapsing. But when I was allowed in at dawn the entire first floor was gutted, charred, and dripping wet. Rebuilding started the same day. Thank God we were properly insured. We reopened the Café in just over two weeks and the restaurant downstairs in less than two months. But in the days after the fire I learned something new about Chez Panisse: it didn't belong to my partners and me as much as it belonged to the people who loved to eat there. We received hundreds of letters and calls and messages from customers who felt like they had suffered a personal loss. It made me realize our responsibility reached outside our doors.

Our very first cookbook, and the first of many intense collaborations. Many of the menus and recipes were part of Jeremiah Tower's legacy; Linda Guenzel, a devoted customer, interviewed me and transcribed my first and second and third thoughts; David Goines designed the book; Patty Curtan and Jean-Pierre Moullé developed dishes; Carolyn Dille tested all the recipes and wrote them up; Jerry Budrick wrote the dedication; and Fritz Streiff did indispensable editorial cleanup work. Fritz has been a creative force in every cookbook project since this one.

The wall between the kitchen and the dining room burned down, and we never rebuilt it. Our customers could see us cooking and walk right into the kitchen if they wanted to.

one tart at a time

CHARLES SHERE *(writer, composer, and director, Pagnol et Cie., Inc.)*: None of the women in the kitchen were more selfless, I think, than my dear wife, Lindsey. She put dessert at the service of the dinner, turning out cakes and tarts and mousses in a little cottage behind the restaurant, running them into the restaurant with an umbrella when it rained. She bicycled the mile to work every day at first; later she drove in her little VW in order to pick up fruit on the way at the Monterey Market.

We were ten years older than Alice and Tom and Jerry when the restaurant opened—still are—and Lindsey's matter-of-factness and serenity helped a lot, I think, in the often high-pitched early days. Also her frugality: growing up on a dairy and fruit farm, the daughter of an Italian immigrant, she knew how to stretch things. In those early days we used to pick acacia blossoms at night, when they were fragrant, to flavor custards: frugality met enterprise.

And our two daughters thought it perfectly natural to take their place, first at Lindsey's side, then moving out to other assignments. Thérèse became a hostess, a lettuce gardener, an early cowriter with Alice; Giovanna moved from the pastry kitchen to the charcuterie across the street, and now writes about food. They were the first second-generation staffers, showing a way for the restaurant to grow into its future.

Most of all, though, Lindsey is defined by her unerring taste, deft hand, patience, farm background, intellectual curiosity, and travel experience, qualities that shaped the restaurant from its early days.

Lindsey was so thrifty that she only wrote notes and lists on old envelopes and scraps of already used leftover paper—on both sides! She planted the seeds of ecological consciousness in the heads of generations of cooks, teaching us all.

grow your own

STEPHEN SINGER (owner, Baker Lane Vineyards and Stephen Singer, Olio): Honnnnnkkk! Honnnnnkkk! Who could that possibly be, leaning on a horn right outside our bedroom window at six A.M.? I soon discover that it is a very short person, and not the usual driver of the car, who is Andrea Crawford, one of the orchestrators of the symphony of greens flourishing in our backyard. No, it is her two-year-old son, Elof, emphatically broadcasting that he is not content to be left in the car while she waters and harvests the tender lettuces that make our garden unique in our neighborhood.

Soon after Alice and I began our romance in the spring of 1982, I remember her saying that she only liked to eat garden lettuces. This comment stood out at the time because I actually didn't know what she meant by "garden" lettuces. I was to find out in a big way.

My green revolution began shortly after we moved into the house on Monterey Avenue. My growing knowledge of garden lettuces came by way of a series of "French intensive" raised beds installed by Andrea, Sibella Kraus, and Thérèse Shere. They were planted in tight formation in our backyard, fitted with hoops to provide support for the plastic sheeting that turned them into mini-greenhouses. At first, they were as confounding as they were visually arresting, presenting an exotic departure from the verdant, if chemically sustained, lawns of my youth. Because my painting studio was in a converted garage adjacent to the rigorously configured lettuce beds, I walked through them many times a day. Eventually, I came to accept the disruptive traffic through our yard that they sometimes generated. And I gradually acclimated to the unlikely reality that I was living, here in our cozy north Berkeley neighborhood, on a version of a family farm. In this case, it was an extended one that had grown out of Chez Panisse.

This version of a family farm that was thriving in our yard expressed many of the values that are essential to our collective appreciation of this most sensible of agricultural models. It was highly efficient, organic in practice, artisanal in output (these lettuces were being eaten by Chez Panisse's diners, after all!), and inspired by talented folks who wanted to reconsider and reignite their relationship to the land that sustains us. Just inside my studio, I was earnestly engaged in a variety of artistic explorations. It wasn't too long before I realized that the lettuce farmers on the other side of the wall were equally motivated by the aesthetic significance of their actions. They were not only cultivating something beautiful, but were also feeding people, engaging in a cultural act, and nurturing an essential part of themselves.

That I became a farmer myself twenty years later now makes perfect sense. Our backyard lettuce farm is where a sense of the possibilities that are inherent in a loving and responsible relationship to the land germinated within me. That sensibility has flourished ever since.

I brought seeds back from France so I could eat my own mesclun salad (*mesclun* means "mixed" in Provençal). It's a mélange of strong-flavored leaves—classically, rocket, young lettuces, chervil, and dandelion.

Cafe Fanny Opens Friday, March 13, 1984

CAFÉ FANNY

ELEANOR BERTINO *(public relations consultant and former director, Slow Food USA)*: Two years before a McDonald's opened near the Spanish Steps in Rome, the event that would spark the Slow Food movement, a Mediterranean version of fast food opened. Café Fanny was intended to be the kind of energetic Italian or Provençal café where you stand at a counter and partake of, say, a prosciutto panini and a glass of wine, or a pastry and an espresso.

In its simplicity, Café Fanny foreshadowed today's pop-up food-cart culture. It opened in March of 1984, and just afterward, because Alice had to leave town for a few weeks, she asked me to hold down the fort along with Edie Ichioka and Judy Rodgers. Word hadn't gotten out yet that we had opened, so the new place felt intensely friendly, because everybody knew everybody else, and the only customers were all, in fact, our families and friends—friends from Chez Panisse, from the baker and wine merchant next door, and from our other suppliers. Within days, though, more neighbors and passersby began to line up at the counter, and before long *le tout Berkeley* was

there, every day. There were complaints at first—the sandwiches were too small, there was no place to sit and linger—and soon the lone bench along the wall was supplemented with a few tables and chairs on the patio. Otherwise, the place hasn't changed much in twenty-seven years. The tight-grained purple-heart-wood bar has darkened, but it hasn't budged.

LAURA MASER *(owner, Café Fanny)*: Friday the 13th, 1984. An auspicious day. How could we evoke the sensuality of France in Berkeley, on San Pablo Avenue of all places? We were young and fearless. Alice overflowed with ideas and enthusiasm. With her new baby, Fanny, on her hip, Alice joined the rest of us (who were also holding babies or small children) and we tasted sandwiches in her kitchen to finalize the menu. Salami, prosciutto, arugula, and mâche, little niçoise olives and cornichons took our senses to southern France and Italy. Big bowls of perfectly creamy café au lait, made with espresso to get the flavor just right. Bowls! The comfort of holding the warm bowl of coffee!

In 1983, Kermit Lynch moved his wine shop to one wing of an L-shaped one-story warehouse about two miles west of Chez Panisse. The other wing was leased to Steve Sullivan's brand-new bakery, the Acme Bread Company. There was a little storefront space wedged between them, and I said to my sister Laura and her husband, Jim Maser, Oh, my goodness, we have to open a little hole-in-the-wall café right there. We'll make a counter out of a couple of barrels and a board and serve Acme bread and wine from Kermit. I named it after my newborn daughter, Fanny, who was named after Pagnol's heroine who outlives Panisse and reunites with her first love, Marius. I just wanted a place where you could go and get a bowl of coffee and milk and a beautiful soft-boiled egg and some toast. At Café Fanny, you still can, all these years later. It's the only other place I've opened besides Chez Panisse.

FROM LEFT, TOP TO BOTTOM: Michael Fuller, Sharon Jones, Nico Monday; Stephen Thomas, Patty Curtan, and Zachary Thomas; Elizabeth Avedisian of the Cheese Board Collective; Jim Maser, Laura Maser, and Colette Maser.

The pasta, pizza, and calzone book was a sisterly collaboration with Patty Curtan (*left*), who wrote the recipes and did the book design, and my old friend Martine Labro (*right*), who did the illustrations. The Café had been open for a couple of years, and I had been thinking a lot about the kind of daily, affordable foods that they eat in the south of France and Italy. We set out to localize them, by seeing them in a Northern California context. The book is full of ideas that are right out of Martine's kitchen garden.

Other friends had children about the same time I had Fanny, and together we had to figure out a balance between work and child care. As Fanny (at left, about eight years old, with her friend Carrie Stefansky on the right) grew up, I began to think about how to teach kids what we had been learning at Chez Panisse. In *Fanny at Chez Panisse* I tried to show where food comes from and what it means with stories they could understand—and recipes they could cook themselves.

FANNY SINGER *(student, writer)*: The old converted house at 1517 Shattuck Avenue has always felt as if it were an extension of the nearby home I occupied with my parents. Some of the earliest photos of me were taken at Chez Panisse. In one, I am swaddled in kitchen towels and nestled in a huge stainless steel salad bowl in the downstairs kitchen. In the background, cooks are peeling beets and onions. This vignette illustrates the lifelong relationship I've had to the restaurant.

Growing up there, I always knew the best places to hide in games of hide-and-seek, exactly how many of the back stairs could be cleared in one leap, and from which shelf in the walk-in I could pilfer cookie dough undetectably. Many of the cooks and waiters assumed informal babysitting roles: Tom Guernsey and I would crouch underneath tables in the dining room for impromptu tea parties; Mary Jo Thoreson would freeze raspberries for me to put on my fingertips as I sat on her pastry counter; and Michele Perrella would teach me how to roll out a pizza while I perched on an overturned plastic dough bucket.

However, I was hardly the only kid navigating the corridors of the restaurant with total familiarity. The sons and daughters of Chez Panisse employees past and present felt equally proprietary about the place. Chez Panisse is often described as a family, and justifiably so: not only has much of the staff been employed there for decades, but

they also have willingly folded their families into the rhythms of the restaurant. Together with Jean-Pierre's daughters, Maud and Elsa, I would cavort around the kitchen and back courtyard until we got in the way. Sharon Jones's sons, Nico and Oliver, were present at every staff party and many meals in between. Staff parties were like family reunions, gathering together generations of cooks, bartenders, and waiters. Everyone was welcome. These congregations have always been elaborate affairs centered on food and regularly take place at Bob Cannard's farm in Sonoma. We children would escape into the wild and edible heaven of the fields until we were lured back by the smell of food or the promise of a softball game.

As a teenager I was roped into employment every summer and given more responsibility every year. Too young to be a busboy, I first worked behind the scenes, prepping ingredients. My memories of those first years in the kitchen are disproportionately about cleaning salt-packed anchovies. How is it possible, I used to wonder, that any restaurant could go through so many smelly fish so fast? For a child with a sense of smell keen enough to deduce the menu from the fragrances still clinging to my mother's clothes when she came home, cleaning anchovies for the summer could have been torture. But the experience was tempered by so many other lessons from the extraordinarily patient cooks with whom

I labored contentedly. No question irritated Mona Talbott, who would find time in the middle of a rush to demonstrate how to cut tissue-thin slices of smoked salmon. And Gilbert Pilgram would stand by while I whisked quarts of oil into egg yolks to make aioli, proffering encouragements in his lilting Mexican accent when my arm felt like it might fall off. The pastry cooks may have been the most patient of all, so tolerant were they of my ineptitude where desserts were concerned. After one week during which 50 percent too many eggs were added to a custard and the molasses was left out of a batch of gingersnaps, no fact of parentage could grant me immunity. I was sent back to the salad station, where I have happily remained, in spirit if not in person, ever since.

Ten years later, many of us who grew up there are still involved in the life of the restaurant. Had you ventured in for dinner last spring, you would have been met by Maud with the warmth of someone welcoming you into her home. In the kitchen, Nico would have been tending the smoldering hearth, turning quail over a grape wood fire. Elsa would have been chopping vegetables—vegetables harvested by Oliver and the other farming apprentices up at Bob Cannard's farm. And a new generation of children is hopping up and down the back stairs, sneaking cherry tomatoes off the shelves, and delighting in spoonfuls of mulberry ice cream.

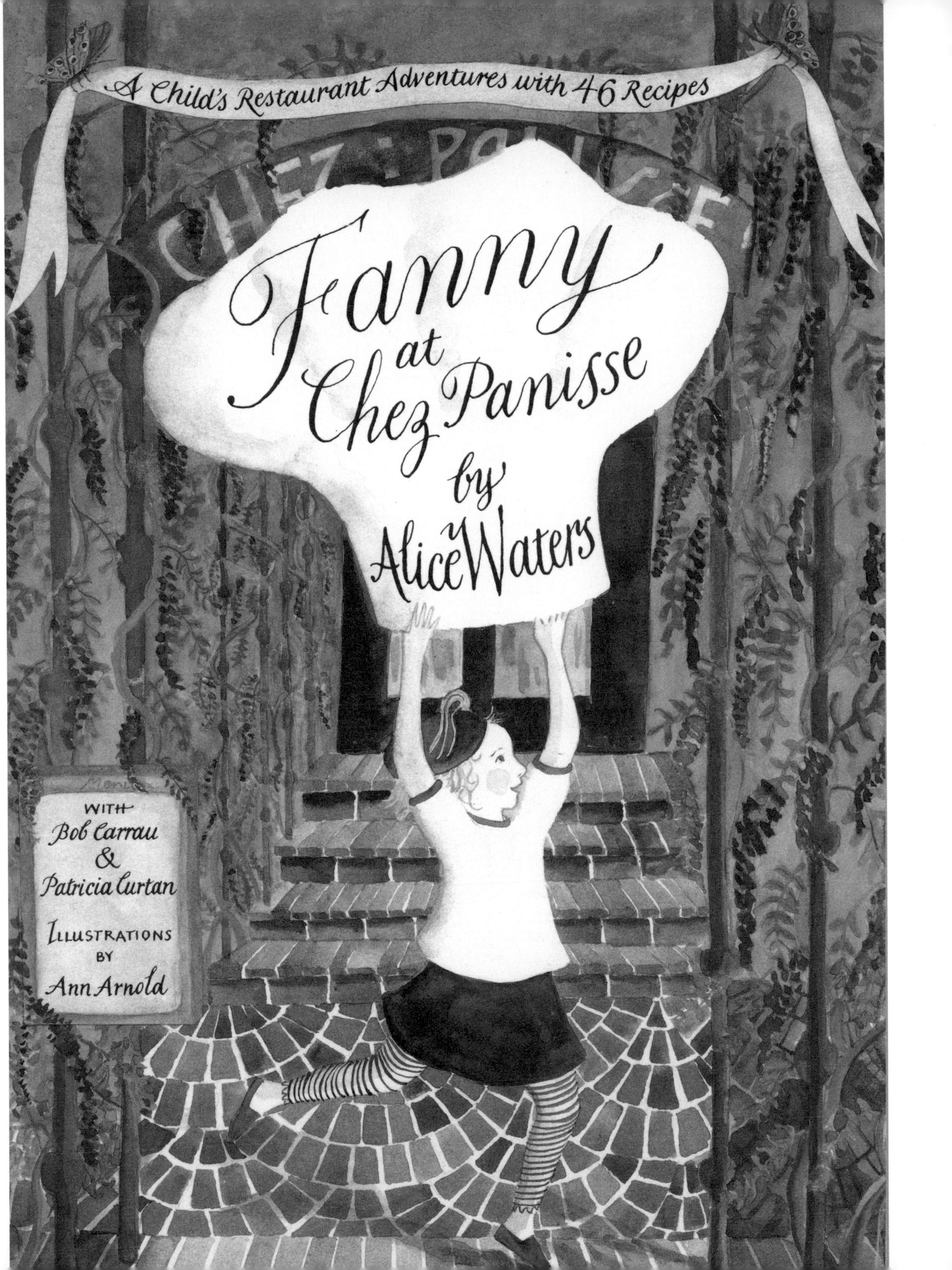

A Child's Restaurant Adventures with 46 Recipes

Fanny at Chez Panisse

by Alice Waters

WITH
Bob Carrau
&
Patricia Curtan

ILLUSTRATIONS
BY
Ann Arnold

CLOCKWISE FROM ABOVE: In the Chez Panisse downstairs kitchen: Paul Bertolli, Seen Lippert, Christopher Lee, and Kees Elfring; Jacques Pépin, Alice, and Paul Bertolli; waiter David Stewart and Alice.

a new palette of flavor

Paul Bertolli wanted to work at Chez Panisse before 1983, but it wasn't until that summer, when I was invited to a lunch party he cooked for Susie Nelson, who'd been a host at Chez Panisse, that I knew he had to be hired. I remember everything he cooked—the *vitello tonnato*, the lamb cooked over fig branches, a prune *semifreddo* with *nocino*— and everything surprised me. He threw open the door to Italian cooking for us, and it all poured in, technique and tradition and ingredients, a whole new palette of flavors.

PAUL BERTOLLI *(owner, Fra' Mani; former chef, Chez Panisse)*: Unquestionably, cooking at Chez Panisse was the most formative experience of my life in food. The menus I wrote over the course of nearly ten years in the downstairs kitchen allowed me the opportunity to conceive and cook an astounding variety of dishes, to work with a crew of brilliant cooks, to handle the rarest produce, to collaborate with foragers and farmers and backyard gardeners and legendary mentors all attracted to the magic that is Chez Panisse. Under the best of circumstances dinner was an improvisation, with all of us tuned to the Chez Panisse ethic of letting the cooking be guided by the ingredients themselves. In this respect Chez Panisse was and still is the model for the best kind of cooking: alive, responsive, transparent, illusively simple. Forty years on, the magic continues. I am still drawn back to the place, now grown resonant with time, where I first found Alice stirring the pot, where my friends and family can gather in the warm glow of the dining room, sharing food that is always delicious and true.

Paul Bertolli and
Seen Lippert
at the Robert
Mondavi Winery.

In 1983 we were invited to appear in the Robert Mondavi Winery's Great Chefs series created by Margrit Biever Mondavi. They thought I was the chef, but of course that wasn't exactly true: Paul Bertolli and Seen Lippert and Lindsey all went with me. Paul made an extraordinary bouillabaisse in the big cauldron and a dish of salmon in gelée with the "cheeks" of multicolored tomatoes. We did most of the cooking outside.

SEEN LIPPERT (cooking teacher, chef): Learning to cook just about anywhere—in a hearth, in someone's backyard, or outside in the middle of New York City—this is what we do. Keeping your grill and open fire alive while it sprinkles or pours rain and creating a makeshift workspace and table can sometimes be a challenge. Alice always makes it fun though, whether it's making 4,000 crêpes in Rockefeller Center, or balancing the huge copper cauldron on the coals so that the whole fishes for the bouillabaisse actually stay in the pot, or begging a neighbor for some of their vine leaves. To have the confidence to take raw, pure ingredients and turn them into a delicious meal (inside or out) is one of the most valuable skills.

Elizabeth David

I finally got a chance to meet and cook for Elizabeth David when she came to stay with her friend Gerald Asher in San Francisco. She dined at Chez Panisse on several occasions (the menu for one of these is on the right). I also had the pleasure of packing picnic lunches for her and Gerald when they went on a trip to Yosemite. I took great pains to assemble a simple meal with some perfect seasonal fruit, a local cheese, a cold bottle of rosé, and a loaf of bread and packed it in a beautiful basket with vintage linen, antique china plates, silverware, and real glass glasses.

SALLY CLARKE (*restaurateur*): For over twenty-five years I have gently (and sometimes not so gently) guided my cooks to imagine that I am sitting on their shoulders as they work. In the same way, I stand in the kitchen, imagining that I have Alice on one shoulder and Elizabeth David on the other. "Would Alice have chosen this to go with that?" "Would Mrs. David have done it like this?" In this way I question every gut reaction and keep a constant check on my decision-making process and on the taste and look of a dish.

My first entry into the sunny world of *Summer Cooking*, *A Book of Mediterranean Food*, and *French Provincial Cooking* was at home in Surrey, at the age of nine or ten. I would read these books with my mother. A recipe would be discussed, ingredients sought, ideas would evolve, and lunch would be prepared, often with an adaptation or two, due to the lack of an item such as an aubergine or olive oil. This was England in the mid-1960s, after all.

Years later, walking into Chez Panisse for the first time, I was surrounded by echoes of evocative passages in those books—in the flowers, the bowls of fruits, the lighting, the linen, the choice of plates. And the menu—it was all about the menu. Appropriate not only for the season, but also in balance with the occasion, in the colors, tastes, and presentation. The style of service was perfect, professional yet totally in love with the act of presenting the most special of foods from the most special of kitchens.

I hold in my mind, as Alice does, images of Mrs. David sitting in our respective restaurants, her beautiful hair tied up in a loose knot, her earrings and necklaces from far-off lands swinging as she spoke. How lucky Alice and I are to have known her and to have received her pretty smiles of appreciation.

MENU

24 September 1988

Brawn of suckling pork with fall salads

Shellfish consomme

Pigeon in verjuice

Fraises des bois

For Elizabeth David *at Chez Panisse*

CHEZ PANISSE
COOKING

—————— *by* ——————

Paul Bertolli with Alice Waters

Photographs by Gail Skoff

Paul Bertolli wrote all but a few pages of *Chez Panisse Cooking*, but the publisher insisted on adding my name to the cover. Paul's great attention to detail and his sensuality permeate the recipes. Unfortunately the magical hand-colored photographs by Gail Skoff appeared in only the hardcover edition. The one on the cover is a close-up of some exquisite root vegetables from the Chino Farm. The one on the opposite page is of pared artichokes in the downstairs kitchen.

extended family

THE CHINO FARM

Everyone from the restaurant who makes the pilgrimage to the Chinos' feels like it's part of their initiation into our extended family. Walking through their fields with the hundreds of rare and heirloom varieties of scores of fruits and vegetables is a priceless education in biodiversity—and beauty. Their vegetables have been sent to our kitchen for over thirty years, ever since my old friend Jean-Pierre Gorin brought me a box of their skinny little French haricots verts. When I first saw them, I thought they were the most dazzlingly beautiful vegetables I had ever seen.

MARK SINGER (writer): . . . a twenty-five-foot-long counter covered with neatly arranged beets (yellow, golden, red, white with red stripes), carrots (white, orange, yellow, red, long-and-tapered, thumb size, in-between), turnips (white, golden, red, black, white-and-purple, round, long), radishes (white, red, red-and-white, purple, pink, daikon, red-fleshed Chinese, green-fleshed Chinese), celeriac, fennel, escarole, white endive, red endive, white cauliflower, Romanesque cauliflower (pale green with a stegosauroid architecture), mibuna, mizuna, bok choy, choi sun, cilantro, French thyme, winter savory, lemon balm, rapini, garlic chives, nasturtiums, basil (lemon, cinnamon, Thai, French, piccolo fino), Vietnamese coriander, Chinese spinach, Chinese long beans, French green beans as slender as candlewicks, purple cabbage, two dozen varieties of lettuce, a tray of lettuce hearts—and that's not all.

The roadside stand officially does business as the Vegetable Shop, but regulars call it the Chinos'. It sits on the periphery of a fifty-six-acre farm twenty-one miles north of San Diego and five miles from the Pacific. Tom Chino, who was born in 1949 and has spent all but four years of his life on the farm, is the youngest of nine children, all nisei—second-generation Japanese Americans. His active business partners are a sister, Kazumi, and two brothers, Koo and Fumio. The world outside the family know Kazumi as Kay, Koo as Frank, and Fumio as Fred.

mochi for the new year

For over fifteen years now, I've gone down to participate in the Chinos' annual New Year's *mochi*-pounding ritual. *Mochi* is the glutinous rice cake that is an obligatory part of New Year's celebrations in Japan. To make it the traditional way requires hours of pounding cooked rice in a giant stone mortar. The Chinos invite their friends, cook three hundred pounds of rice, and everyone can take turns wielding the big mallets.

CLOCKWISE FROM TOP RIGHT: Kagami *mochi*, the traditional Japanese New Year's decoration; (*from left*) Nina MacConnel, Alice, Kay Chino, Nancy Silverton, and Tom Chino. OPPOSITE, CLOCKWISE FROM TOP LEFT: Tom and Kay Chino; Hideo Chino; making *mochi*.

taking care of our friends

The Aid and Comfort events—which were fund-raising benefits for several AIDS organizations—were an intense collective response to the enormous personal losses we all were suffering during those years. Our beloved partner Tom Guernsey was diagnosed before the first event and died before the second. The kind of collaboration these events required was something beyond anything we had ever attempted before, both in size and in complexity—the artists and musicians, the logistics, the planning.

AID & COMFORT

THE SAN FRANCISCO RESTAURANT BENEFIT
FOR PEOPLE FIGHTING AIDS

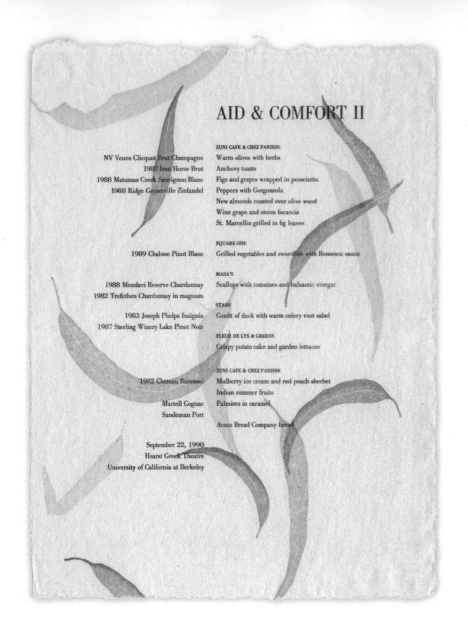

AID & COMFORT II

	ZUNI CAFE & CHEZ PANISSE
NV Veuve Clicquot Brut Champagne	Warm olives with herbs
1987 Iron Horse Brut	Anchovy toasts
1988 Matanzas Creek Sauvignon Blanc	Figs and grapes wrapped in prosciutto
1988 Ridge Geyserville Zinfandel	Peppers with Gorgonzola
	New almonds roasted over olive wood
	Wine grape and onion focaccia
	St. Marcellin grilled in fig leaves

	SQUARE ONE
1989 Chalone Pinot Blanc	Grilled vegetables and swordfish with Romescu sauce

	MASA'S
1988 Mondavi Reserve Chardonnay	Scallops with tomatoes and balsamic vinegar
1982 Trefethen Chardonnay in magnum	

	STARS
1983 Joseph Phelps Insignia	Confit of duck with warm celery root salad
1987 Sterling Winery Lake Pinot Noir	

	FLEUR DE LYS & GREENS
	Crispy potato cake and garden lettuces

	ZUNI CAFE & CHEZ PANISSE
1982 Chateau Rieussec	Mulberry ice cream and red peach sherbet
	Indian summer fruits
Martell Cognac	Palmiers in caramel
Sandeman Port	
	Acme Bread Company bread

September 22, 1990
Hearst Greek Theatre
University of California at Berkeley

After the Aid and Comfort benefits, all the big events we did were always about more than just Chez Panisse and its community; they were about the concerns of a wider and more dangerous world. For Aid and Comfort II we gathered at the Greek Theater at the University of California, which is a replica of the amphitheater at Epidaurus in Greece, a place where people came together to learn how to live with tragedy.

PATRICIA UNTERMAN *(restaurateur and writer)*: The two groundbreaking Aid and Comfort events grew out of the personal tragedy that affected practically everyone in San Francisco in the mid-eighties. What happened to my partner Robert Flaherty was miserably typical.

Robert was an associate at a big San Francisco law firm when I first met him in 1969. Three years later he quit and came out. In 1979 we opened Hayes Street Grill. He found the location in one day, structured the deal that got us started, designed the dining room and ran the front of the house, all while being swept up in the euphoria of being freely and openly gay. In 1985, he contracted AIDS. At the time, no one really knew what that meant except that it was fatal; people, gay and straight, were terrified about becoming infected. He died in March 1987, exactly fifteen months after diagnosis, like so many others.

In shock, we were helpless and miserable, as people we loved kept dying relentlessly. The restaurant community in particular was ravaged. Though no one understood how to stop the march of death at that point, the one thing we could do to relieve our own sadness was to raise public consciousness about what was really going on in the face of fear, misinformation, and paranoia. So many around us needed care and compassion. Almost spontaneously, a group of restaurant and food people started meeting to figure out what to do. Aid and Comfort was born.

The group threw two blow-out fund-raising events that called upon the most talented people in the food and art worlds. Alice was at her most visionary in conceiving them. In 1987 we took over a pier in Fort Mason. Eiko Ishioka designed the space. Restaurants set up temporary kitchens to cook for a thousand. An army of volunteer wait-

ers served. The finest wines flowed. Tom Luddy produced a sexy show starring Linda Ronstadt, the Kronos Quartet, and the San Francisco Ballet. Fine artists collaborated with chefs to create a limited edition letterpress portfolio of illustrated recipes to sell. Private and corporate donations poured in. This seminal, heartfelt, and very high-profile event almost singlehandedly changed community and national attitudes about AIDS.

We mounted a second Aid and Comfort three years later in October of 1990 at the Greek Theater in Berkeley with a big show featuring Philip Glass, Herbie Hancock, John Adams, and Laurie Anderson. Restaurants prepared thousands of box lunches and a sit-down dinner for five hundred. Volunteers spent months working out every detail. But one of the things we couldn't control was the weather. It poured during the event, and we wept for all those who were not there, and ultimately felt better.

Parsi new year

I love rituals that punctuate the year with fresh reasons to gather friends around the table; and I love gathering fresh influences and inspirations into our kitchens.

NILOUFER ICHAPORIA KING *(cook, writer, food scholar):* A thousand years after our ancestors left Persia, Parsis in India continue to observe the spring equinox on March 21. We call it Jamshedji Navroz to distinguish it from our second New Year in August. Ever since I came to the United States, Navroz in spring has become my favorite annual festival, to be celebrated with auspicious, chalk-stenciled decorations, throngs of friends, masses of flowers, extravagant food. Alice, who likes all New Years, came to a couple of our Navroz routs before suggesting we move the celebration over to

Chez Panisse. We had our first Parsi New Year dinner there on March 20, 1989. Earlier that month, I went to Alice with a list of things to consider, having cooked through all of the possibilities for weeks. Looking over the list she said, "I want all of it!" All of it got wrestled into the turmeric pigment-dipped menu you see on the opposite page. Later, I heard Alice say that this first Parsi New Year menu was like the unedited *Apocalypse Now.* By then I'd learned that "I want all of it!" really meant, "Just do it."

We did our next dinner in 1992, then again in 1994, resuming in 2000 and every year since, our fifteenth dinner the year of Chez Panisse's fortieth birthday. Like many recurring events, this Navroz dinner has developed its own traditions, many of them Parsi, others decidedly idiosyncratic and quirky. At first, I missed the party at home, but now, when I work with the same familiar colleagues in the kitchen and look into a garland-bedecked dining room filled with friends, I realize that it's a family celebration still.

નવરોજ મુબારક

Parsi New Year's Eve · March 20, 1989 · Chez Panisse

Cucumber pickles, masala cashews & green mango
Ritual dal

Brain and green chutney fritters, panir fritters
Fried taro leaf rolls & tomato chutney

Lobster with coconut milk & semolina dhokla

Grilled quail, nargisi kebabs and rice
Cauliflower with five seeds, masala stuffed eggplant
Bottle gourd in yoghurt & spring greens with ginger

Pomegranate and melon ices
Nankhatai and date pastries

Parsi tea with lemon grass and mint

Navroz Mubarak!   Niloufer Ichaporia, chef

Chef Cal Peternell prepares food for the Café in the early nineties.

Chez Panisse

farmers' market
ON SHATTUCK AVENUE

Chez Panisse has always been across the street from the Cheese Board, a collective cheese shop and bakery. Next door, for over ten years, was Pig-by-the-Tail, the charcuterie founded by Victoria Kroyer (now Victoria Wise) after she left Chez Panisse in 1973. We felt close to both businesses. I always wanted to get across the street easily. I even dreamed of a pedestrian overpass that looked like the Rialto Bridge in Venice—either that or close the street. For our twentieth birthday, I got my wish. We received permission from the city to divert traffic and hold a street fair for one Sunday in August. We invited our purveyors to set up food booths and market stalls down both sides of the street. One of the ranchers brought live farm animals for a little petting zoo. Outside the restaurant, we served watermelon-lime punch and I signed books and posters. Paul Bertolli made roast pork sandwiches. The Café cooked grilled corn. Niloufer Ichaporia King served fresh fruit with Indian spices. David Goines's poster, above, depicts a waitress, Jennifer Caminetti, under a Carmen Miranda hat.

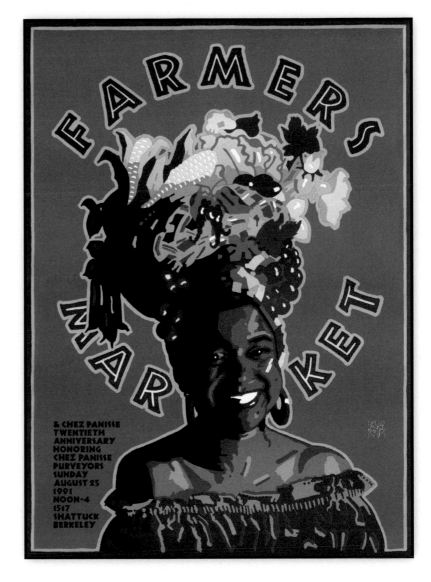

celebrating the producers

It was the perfect farmers' market. Not only did the purveyors show you what they had, but they gave you little tastes, too— warm tacos, corn on the cob, fresh fruit seasoned with chile pepper, spit-roasted pork sandwiches. Our only worry was that there wouldn't be enough. We thought we might draw two or three thousand people, but the street was mobbed. Estimates of the crowd were as high as 14,000.

CLOCKWISE FROM TOP: Catherine Brandel and David Tanis; Kip Mesirow and his son, Wesley; unidentified musicians; Ginger, Jerry, and Deborah Budrick; and Tom, Chris, and Janet Lee. OPPOSITE, FROM TOP: Bob Cannard; (*from left*) Mike Tusk, Ramona d'Viola, Gilbert Pilgram, Russell Moore, Tony Brush, Deborah Sigler, Suzanne Goin, Jon Helquist.

RUSSELL MOORE *(chef, restaurateur)*: The time of the twentieth birthday was an important moment in my cooking career. I had been working at Chez Panisse for a few years and I still had so much to learn about cooking, working, food, and farms. Mike Tusk, Suzanne Goin, Gilbert Pilgram, and I were all cooks at the same time. We all looked up to Tony Brush. We tried to show off by making each other interesting pastas and sandwiches for our staff meals. Tony was relentless with criticism and praise. He once actually told me, "That's the worst pasta I've ever had."

Working at Chez Panisse taught me the value of working in a critical environment; working with Mike, Suzanne, Gilbert, and Tony made it fun. We were constantly being challenged but had the luxury of not being in charge—we were just trying to be good cooks. Now we all have restaurants—except Tony. I think he is too much of a perfectionist. I still remember the pasta I made him and I still get nervous with he comes to my restaurant, Camino. Luckily, we don't make pasta at Camino—I leave that to Mike at Quince.

SIBELLA KRAUS *(writer, food activist)*: The law had only recently been changed to permit produce to be sold without meeting standard packing and labeling requirements, and there were only a few farmers' markets in the entire Bay Area. To provide a showcase for new products and a place for growers and consumers to meet, I founded the Tasting of Summer Produce. Originally started as an intimate gathering for farmers and restaurateurs at Greens Restaurant, the Tasting moved first to the Robert Mondavi Winery and then to the Oakland Museum, where for five years it was a sold-out event with thousands of attendees. Pressure was mounting for the University of California to develop a sustainable agriculture program and for the U.S. Department of Agriculture to develop a national organic program. Communities everywhere were beginning to clamor for their own farmers' markets. The local, sustainable food movement was starting to go mainstream.

defined by the seasons

OPPOSITE: Cal Peternell (*left*) and Russell Moore, with a pig from Paul Willis's ranch, Iowa.

ALICE WATERS

CHEZ PANISSE
VEGETABLES

This book was designed with the vegetables in alphabetical order so that when you came home from the farmers' market, you could look up what you just bought and right away figure out something wonderful to do with it. We put a winter vegetable on the cover on purpose, to remind people that the winter vegetables can be as glorious and enticing as any summer ones.

CAL PETERNELL *(chef, Chez Panisse)*: While a few of the cooks at Chez Panisse are vegetarians, and a vegan or two has occasionally grazed through, the majority are eager meat-cutters, -cookers, and -eaters. But we all share a passion for the seasonal arrival of our glorious local fruits and vegetables—gold and green romano beans in the summer, squashes to roast in autumn, hearty winter greens, tender spring asparagus. Anticipating this cycle keeps our senses from complacency and our minds and palates fresh.

There are the victorious years when spring starts with sweet peas from Yolo County and morels brought to the kitchen door from the snowmelt slopes of Shasta. There is the summer made especially fine because the tomatoes, which last year were left bland by a late-season coolness, seem more bright and fragrant. The way the peppers peak in a sunset-colored flameout in those last weeks of October, just before the cold rains start and put an end to warm weather crops. The year when the artichokes just aren't as good. The year when the little white turnips couldn't be better. And those rare, nervous wintry weeks when it seems that nothing is in season, when celery and rutabaga suddenly hold fresh appeal—and then tiny, sweet tangerines appear, and we know it's going to be all right.

We are linked—farms and farmers, kitchens and cooks—waiting to receive and respond to the season's bounty or bust.

a farm of our own

In 1985 my dad devoted himself to finding a farm that we could work with year-round, growing the produce we wanted, in the quantities we needed. The farm would have to be organic and no more than ninety minutes away by car, at most. He interviewed more than a hundred farmers before he winnowed the candidates down to eighteen, and then to four. He made a slide-show presentation of the final four for me, the chefs, and the board of directors, but by then the winner was all but foreordained. It had to be Bob Cannard. It took us several years to work out the kinks of our relationship, but by the early nineties things were running smoothly, as they still are today. Twice a week Dhondup Karpo, our farm driver, drives our van to Bob's Sonoma County farm, which is about an hour away. He unloads our vegetable waste onto Bob's compost, helps pick vegetables, and loads them into the van for the return trip. Cooks visit regularly, too, and the chefs telephone Bob several times a week to get an idea of what's on the way and to make suggestions for the future.

RUSSELL MOORE (chef, restaurateur): Chez Panisse's most far-reaching contribution to the restaurant world is raising a generation of cooks who don't know another way of buying produce except directly from farmers. It's a lot easier now, because there are systems in place, but I remember when we first started working with Bob. I was the first cook to be sent to the farm. I had no idea what I was doing, I couldn't tell a weed from an herb, I would get caked in mud, and I was afraid of every bug that jumped on me—but I didn't care. I was so smitten with Bob, I didn't care how much of a hassle it was—I got to be a part of his farm. I got to taste Bob's dirt (which tastes great) and try to keep up with his talk of broad-spectrum minerals and companion plants (as he calls his weeds, some of which he plants on purpose). Back at the restaurant, I got to cook the most vibrant vegetables I'd ever seen. When I opened my restaurant Camino, I couldn't get any produce from him. I felt like there was a hole in my menu. Bob's herbs alone can transform a dish.

walking the farm

Bob Cannard, from Maira Kalman's visual column "And the Pursuit of Happiness," for the *New York Times*.

DAVID TANIS *(chef, writer)*:

early morning going to the farm
driving north from Berkeley on the freeway
west over the water Richmond bridge heading inland
yellow grass-covered hills dotted with clusters of live oaks
the road's getting smaller
dairy cattle are lounging in the fields
this former Sonoma wilderness now cluttered
with housing developments and boutique wineries
this sleepy farmland once famous for apples and prunes
now sprouts grapevines and weekend homes
even Bob's rented farmland surrounded by upscale estates

turning up the drive you begin to feel far from the world
a swath of wilderness remains a quiet little farm is growing
slowing along the gravel road and pulling up next to a tractor
you always get out and start walking the farm by yourself
sometimes encountering Bob along the way sometimes not
it's a circular walk you know by heart like coming home
past the tool and seed barn are zucchini this year
little rondes de Nice healthy and full of blossoms
the walnut tree on the right has green fruit
for pickling or making *nocino*
crossing the culvert inspecting all the fields seeing
what's been growing
what is growing
what will be growing

the cardoons are in repose until next fall
walking up toward the compost tea operation
the crushed rocks are full of minerals
a dozen side-by-side plantations make
a giant carpet of muted colors

hundreds of strapping young tomato plants are setting flowers
next to a thousand new garlic sprouts
next to stretches of lacy fennel and deep green chard

down the hill across a little footbridge over the creek
damp air perfumed by wild bay laurel
past the vegetable-washing sinks and packing shed
boxes of lettuces carrots potatoes beets turnips
covered in wet burlap waiting in the shade
the little orchard of apricots
was storm-battered and heavily pruned last year
this year a meager crop but the peach trees are hardy
and the lemon trees give year-round
the cherries are just starting
fava beans are over the first green beans are ready
tasting everything along the way
here are the herbs
masses of lemon verbena
hedges of rosemary thyme and savory in great bushy patches
fragrant sage borders a scruffy vineyard of table grapes
the boysenberries melt in your mouth

arugula does well behind the old turkey barn
chervil likes the shade of big chestnut trees
the cilantro is flowering and going to seed
leafy comfrey thrives in the beds closest to Bob's house
you share on the picnic table
a pot of strong coffee
a little breakfast
and a hand-rolled organic tobacco cigarette

now back to work

with Bob Cannard

grandes dames

Edna Lewis was born in 1916, in a Virginia Piedmont farming community called Freetown that had been founded by her grandfather and other freed slaves in 1865. In 1976, she published a great classic cookbook, *The Taste of Country Cooking*, which recaptures a culinary past of great dignity and purity. Her life-long commitment to preserving her southern cultural heritage is an inspiration to all who believe we best honor the past by preserving both our biodiversity and our cultural diversity. It was a deep honor to me to get to know her in the last decades of her life (she died in 2006). We cooked together at several benefits in New York City, and I was always struck by her calm determination, her quiet competence, and her generosity of spirit. In contrast to the other celebrity chefs with their brigades of helpers and elaborate presentations, she would stand alone, or with her friend Scott Peacock, rolling out pastry and baking irresistible pies, one at a time. She was a living national treasure.

BELOW: Miss Edna Regina Lewis (*left*) with Marion Cunningham in New York City. Both were mentors, guides, and confidantes.

# of American cooking

At fifty, her children grown, Marion Cunningham had been rescued from suburbia—and agoraphobia—by James Beard, who made her his cooking-class assistant and recommended her for the job of writing an all-new edition of an American classic, *The Fannie Farmer Cookbook*, which occupied her for seven years. Her support for Chez Panisse never flagged. She loved coming to dinner with her husband, Robert, who claimed to be a meat-and-potatoes man, but who could be fooled into trying just about anything. From her first visit, Marion appreciated what we were trying to do. She liked to quote James Beard, who said of us, "This is not a real restaurant," which we all took as a great compliment. Marion was so plainspoken and accessible that she could talk to anybody, anywhere. She loved the food world, which gave her the opportunity to be mother confessor to a wide circle of all different sorts of people. It was through her that I kept up with everybody in that world: James Beard; Cecilia Chiang, who ran The Mandarin, a wonderful San Francisco restaurant, and who also became a friend; Michael James and Billy Cross, who ran the Great Chefs events at the Mondavi Winery; Danny Kaye; Edna Lewis and Scott Peacock; and far too many other chefs and food writers to mention.

PEGGY KNICKERBOCKER *(food writer)*: Marion was unapologetic about being an all-American cook. She loved to collect old-fashioned and unfashionable recipes, and to encourage people to try them. She could teach anybody to make pie crust: from grown-ups so clueless that they expected to find softened butter in the supermarket dairy case to children who had never sat down to a family meal; and from prize-winning food journalists to Michelin-starred chefs.

Cooking was never a lofty or pretentious activity to her. I remember Marion's delight—and Alice's disapproval—when she was appointed the official spokeswoman of the California Iceberg Lettuce Commission. "Why not?" she said, "I love a crisp wedge with Thousand Island dressing." When Alice found out that you could get organically grown iceberg lettuce, she surprised Marion with a whole case, and Marion loved it.

home cooking

Marion celebrated many of her birthdays at Chez Panisse, but for her seventieth birthday in 1992 we pulled out all the stops and organized a surprise party at the Robert Mondavi Winery for her and over a hundred of her friends. We worked on it for months, and somehow Marion never found out. Billy Cross had filled the hall with enormous white *Phalaenopsis* orchid plants in full bloom (her favorite flower), which he had been growing for six months. We planned a menu that included Dungeness crab toasts, chicken pot pies with wild mushrooms and green peas, pickled beets, an iceberg lettuce salad, and eighteen different cakes. Ten years later we helped organize another birthday party for her and eighty friends, this time at Chez Panisse. On this occasion, we came up with eighty desserts, including many wonderful cakes, a towering *croquembouche*, and little limes filled with sherbet. But for the salad I didn't want to serve iceberg lettuce again and chose instead an Italian chicory variety called *pane di zucchero* ("sugarloaf"). But it wasn't sweet enough! Marion couldn't help but be a little smug. "As if we ever needed proof that iceberg lettuce is necessary," she said.

Menu for Marion's Birthday

PAN-FRIED SKATE WINGS
TURNIP & TURNIP GREEN SOUP
GRILLED DUCK BREAST
· BLOOD ORANGE SAUCE
· BUCKWHEAT NOODLES
GARDEN SALAD
PISTACHIO ICE CREAM SANDWICHES

CHEZ PANISSE : 4 FEBRUARY 1984

PEGGY KNICKERBOCKER (*food writer*): I don't know how she did it, but Marion never looked as if she was a woman who loved desserts as much as she did. She especially loved cakes: coffee crunch cake, almond cake, coconut cake, carrot cake. Nevertheless, clothes hung on her tall frame with an inimitable elegance. Her eyes were the bluest of blues, and her white hair, pulled back into a chic ponytail, showed off her high cheekbones. When I'd meet her for a monthly dinner at Chez Panisse, she'd tell me about all the baking she'd been doing all day, but she still perked up when the dessert menu appeared. In fact, when Alice knew Marion was coming, she'd instruct the pastry chefs to "Marionize" things, making them a little bit sweeter.

fruit has the power to go right to the heart of our being

DEBORAH MADISON *(writer)*: I remember my first meal at Chez Panisse as if I just got up from the table. It was summer, it was 1977, and it was dinner with my husband. I ate food I had long imagined but never tasted. Our plates looked as if a dog had licked them clean. Our enthusiasm was rewarded with a sampling of desserts—a tart of fragrant strawberries, a simple raspberry tart, and shards of a chewy wonder of an almond tart. These were the best desserts I had ever eaten. There were tears.

A week later, I found myself working in Lindsey's corner of the kitchen. Until then my world had been made up of roots, tubers, leafy greens, beige grains, and shiny beans. Under Lindsey's guidance, a seismic shift occurred. In place of potatoes, aromatic Babcock peaches and red and golden raspberries. In winter, Lavender Gems, blood oranges, pale gold pummelos. Bitter almonds, butternuts, and wild Missouri pecans. Passion fruits, red-fleshed Adriatic figs, perfumed muscat grapes—a lush, sensual, seasonal parade of fruits. I saw how respectfully Lindsey handled them and used them so their subtle magic was revealed. Many were gleaned from the backyard gardens of Alice's friends, plucked from Lindsey's family's farm, or gathered from trees of friends of the restaurant. Small cartons of *fraises des bois* were brought to the back door, and handfuls of violets, branches of almond blossoms, masses of perfumed roses, all pressed into the service of dessert, every fruit, petal, and nut a treasure. Fruit trumped vegetables for me that year.

The back door is no longer the only portal for such tender treasures, but the world of commercial fruit continues to destroy fruits' innocent sensual pleasures. The aroma is gone. Acidity is being bred out. Young people are said to prefer crisp, sweet fruit that doesn't drip. Lindsey and Alice knew the difference. They had the courage, and the ability, to make dessert a single Arctic Rose nectarine. What can I say but thank you. And please, carry on.

I was never very excited about fruit when I was a child, because I associated fruit with canned fruit cocktail. I had no idea what an extraordinary, exquisite joy it is to eat a tree-ripened peach or perfectly ripe golden raspberries picked off bushes in my own backyard. I never imagined I would grow up to prefer plain fruit over any other dessert.

KELSIE KERR *(writer, former chef, Chez Panisse)*: What was it like, working in the kitchen downstairs? Refreshingly different! We were adamant: make the best food from the best ingredients to best please the diners. That motivation generated a fantastic atmosphere of creativity and collaboration. Each afternoon the chef and the cooks gathered to discuss the day's menu, which was viewed merely as a guideline to be influenced by whatever was at hand, the weather, and everyone's two cents' worth. As the day progressed, while our hands were busy shelling beans or boning squab, our minds were occupied with conversations distilling our rifling of culinary texts and visits to farms, farmers' markets, and faraway places. Our conversations were a floating think tank for future dishes and a crucible for reviewing and critiquing past meals. All the time the chef circulated, discussing flavors and helping move forward whatever was falling behind.

Tasters were the culmination of this open studio of learning and innovation. Each dish, prepared by its creator just before service, was tasted and discussed by us all—and in the end, it never failed. The whole was always greater than the sum of its parts. It really was fun. Sure, it was hard and hot and tedious, as any kitchen can be. But we were switched on and engaged, and all in a shared state of collaborative creativity.

My path has led me out of the restaurant and into the world of teaching and text. My days are now filled with translating that lively collaboration, that love and respect for ingredients and intuition, from the kitchen to the classroom or the page. Sometimes I am nostalgic for that daily immersion in such dynamic camaraderie. But I find it still: at the farmers' market, chatting with farmers; at the table, dining with friends and colleagues; and of course working at the occasional feasting event that brings us all back together.

Both the fruit and vegetable books were illustrated with Patty Curtan's incomparable linoleum cuts. Kelsie Kerr (*above*), who had become one of the downstairs chefs, wrote recipes for both books and was especially instrumental in completing *Chez Panisse Fruit*.

pleasure of work
CAFÉ LIFE

The watercolor (*opposite*) by Gaston Barret is an illustration for a 1958 limited edition of Pagnol's play *Marius.* I had it photographed and enlarged to poster size because it was a perfect depiction of what I wanted to be happening in the Café— people meeting, having a little meal and a great conversation.

KHALIL MUJADEDY *(craftsman, maintenance director, Chez Panisse)*: When I arrived in America from Afghanistan in the mid-eighties, I came empty-handed, but with high hopes of starting my life over again. The moment I arrived, I began my search for employment. I walked into Chez Panisse, and luckily, they offered me a position, which I accepted in the blink of an eye, not knowing that I would be spending nearly thirty years of my life working there.

The Chez Panisse family is full of fresh, exquisite, and loving souls. I instantly formed strong bonds, particularly with Alice, who is an unfathomably remarkable woman. Since the very start of my employment, I have strived to work wholeheartedly for Chez Panisse, and for dearest Alice, as well. For all these years, never once did I dread going to work. I see it like this: Chez Panisse is one united and loving family. It puts a smile on my heart to have been, and still be, so blessed to belong to this family.

CHEZ:PANISSE
HOUSE WHITE
1 9 8 2
SHENANDOAH VALLEY
OF CALIFORNIA
SAUVIGNON BLANC
CLOCKSPRING VINEYARDS

PRODUCED & BOTTLED BY
K A R L Y   W I N E S
P L Y M O U T H · C A
ALCOHOL 13% BY VOLUME

"Good wine is a necessity of life to me."

Thomas Jefferson

We opened with three wines on the wine list: a Fumé Blanc and a Gamay from Robert Mondavi Winery and, by the glass, a 1959 Château Suduiraut. Since then, we have collaborated with some of the pioneers of winemaking in California. We have done dinners with Paul Draper of Ridge Vineyards, and every year we celebrate a week-long Zinfandel festival with wines from over twenty local wineries.

STEPHEN SINGER *(owner, Baker Lane Vineyards and Stephen Singer, Olio)*: I was delighted to assume authority over the wine program at Chez Panisse, but it wasn't immediately clear what the job entailed. Most restaurants require that wines be bought in a cost-efficient and food-friendly manner; that is, not in conflict with the general orientation of the menu. But given the philosophically purposeful bent that Chez Panisse has always pursued, something more should be in play. The need to balance Chez Panisse's philosophical goals with economic demands helped define the wine buyer's responsibilities.

We relied on an insight intrinsic to the appreciation of wine itself. Kermit Lynch, a wise and essential mentor, helped me appreciate (just as Richard Olney and Lucien Peyraud had) that the overwhelming strength (or weakness) of a given wine was found in its balance—that is, how gracefully its textural, acidic, aromatic, and alcoholic components married.

Evaluating quality, character, balance, trueness to type, the producer's commitment to responsible agriculture, the geographical balance of the list, and the connections of the producer to the Chez Panisse community—all these considerations were factored into the wine-buying process. While the lattermost of these, community connections, may be the most elusive, this ultimately proved to be the most significant. The restaurant and wine worlds are notably alike in their relationship-driven nature. Chez Panisse has chosen to exercise its prerogative of voting loudly with its wine dollars, embracing a commonwealth of purpose and balancing cultural aspirations with social responsibility, as soberly and thoughtfully as we can.

November Lunch for Richard Olney

Fennel, cepes, Parmesan cheese
and white truffle salad

Charcoal-grilled black sea bass

Saffron risotto

Spit-roasted veal and
straw potatoes with chanterelles

Garden salad

Cheese

Yquem

Chez Panisse 11 : 16 : 86

"Eating is an agricultural act." Wendell Berry

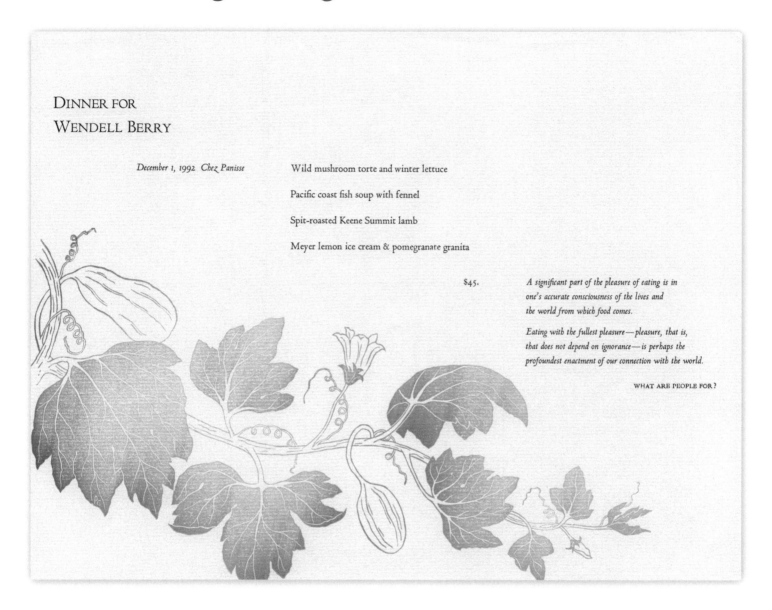

DINNER FOR
WENDELL BERRY

December 1, 1992 Chez Panisse

Wild mushroom torte and winter lettuce

Pacific coast fish soup with fennel

Spit-roasted Keene Summit lamb

Meyer lemon ice cream & pomegranate granita

$45.

A significant part of the pleasure of eating is in one's accurate consciousness of the lives and the world from which food comes.

Eating with the fullest pleasure—pleasure, that is, that does not depend on ignorance—is perhaps the profoundest enactment of our connection with the world.

WHAT ARE PEOPLE FOR?

WENDELL BERRY *(writer, farmer):* We humans, if we are lucky, spend a lot of time eating. To waste so large a portion of our lives on bad food or bad company is a sort of tragedy. I think all of us know this intuitively, but to teach us to know it explicitly has been the purpose of Alice Waters and Chez Panisse. They do not teach us this by little lectures or signs on the wall, but rather by finding the best available food and surrounding it with the kindnesses of good cooking, good taste (in all senses), friendly greeting, and making welcome.

On December 1, 1992, Wallace and Mary Stegner, Jane Vandenberg, Jack Shoemaker, Tanya Berry, and I had the happiness of sitting down together at Chez Panisse to a din-ner of the most wholehearted excellence. Of the thousands of meals I have eaten since then, most of them necessarily forgotten, I remember this one in detail because of the food of course, because of the wine, which I believe came from the estimable wine merchant Kermit Lynch, because of the setting and the company. I have remembered that evening also because it was the last time I saw my friend and teacher, Wallace Stegner, who died the next April.

The Stegners, who were getting on in years then and had a driver waiting, left early. The other four of us stayed on, talking with Kermit Lynch and his wife, Gail Skoff, who were at the table next to ours. And so our dinner ended pleasantly and lingeringly, just as it should have.

25th anniversary

AUGUST 1996

STEPHEN THOMAS *(printmaker; director, Oxbow School)*: From the start it was impressive that Chez Panisse cared about the total experience, not just the food. Lighting, flowers, menus were all components of the meal. Most people think of menus as pieces of paper that won't be looked at again after the first moment. But just as everything that landed on the plate was considered, so was every element of the menus. Good typography, letterpress printing, fine papers—these were basic elements of the everyday menus on the table. For special events, a new level was often achieved, although many of the menus ended up under the table, with a footprint obscuring one of the courses. Over time, the menus became "collectible," a concept far beyond their makers' expectations. The printers, calligraphers, and designers relished the chance to tell a good story in their own patois and to bring some of the spirit of the meal to the eyes before it landed on the palate. Here's to all the printers and all their menus!

How on earth were we going to celebrate twenty-five years? We decided to have six birthday dinners instead of one: one night for chefs and restaurateurs, one for our extended family and former staff, one for purveyors and growers, one for movie people and artists, one for wine people, and one for our oldest and best customers. Patty Curtan designed a new set of menu covers for us, which we still use.

The Chez Panisse Foundation envisions a school curriculum and school lunch program where growing, cooking, and sharing food at the table empowers students to care about what they eat and where their food comes from, and to build a sustainable future.

To celebrate our twenty-fifth birthday, we created a foundation to raise money for a project that had begun two years before at our neighborhood middle school. The Edible Schoolyard had originally been funded by three generous donors—Susie Tompkins Buell, the Robert Mondavi Foundation, and The Center for Ecoliteracy—but when I realized we needed additional support, I knew it was time to enlist the friends of the restaurant. The Edible Schoolyard was a call to action, creating a visionary model of edible education. Our goal was, and remains, to provide universal free lunch for students of every grade in public schools, centered around a hands-on curriculum. It would incorporate a school garden, a kitchen classroom, and a lunchroom, where students and teachers would cook and eat together. All academic subjects would be enriched by this collaborative and inspiring experience: it would be a lab for life sciences, a tool for learning math, a living lesson in social sciences and history. Children would be brought into a transformative relationship with food by learning the values of stewardship, nourishment, and discussion at the table.

an edible schoolyard takes root

The Edible Schoolyard was inspired by The Garden Project at the San Francisco County Jail. In 1982 Cathrine Sneed had started teaching prisoners organic gardening. The food they grew was donated to homeless shelters' kitchens. Many of Cathrine's students were saying that they'd prefer life in jail, if they could keep gardening, to life on the outside. So in 1992 Cathrine founded The Garden Project, a gardening program for ex-convicts and parolees. The Garden Project incorporated everything that's important about food: growing and harvesting, cooking and serving, and sitting down and eating together, with flowers from the garden on the table. Coincidentally, Neil Smith, the enlightened principal of Martin Luther King, Jr., Middle School, had challenged me to help him create a school program that would enrich and nourish his students' lives. Well, if The Garden Project transformed the lives of ex-convicts, think of what it could do for schoolchildren! With the help of teachers like Phoebe Tanner and Beth Sonnenberg and parents like Beebo Thurman, The Edible Schoolyard grew into being. Over the past sixteen years I've witnessed a magical metamorphosis as the school has changed from a campus tagged with graffiti to a place where students gather under the ramada of a garden classroom.

"Approach love and cooking with

reckless abandon."
The Dalai Lama

I was told I should stand in front of the restaurant and greet the Dalai Lama with flowers. Carrie was trying to find a rare Himalayan variety of I can't remember what flower, and she was late, so I was on the sidewalk without flowers in my hand when the Berkeley police rode up on bicycles to cordon off the street. At the last minute Carrie ran in the back door with the flowers and got them to me in the nick of time. I asked the Dalai Lama if he cooked. He said that when he was young his German guardian had tried to show him how to deep-fry dumplings, but when a droplet of hot oil hit his arm he was never allowed to cook again.

"For days, the Tibetans on the restaurant's staff were in a state of almost delirious alert and anticipation." Orville Schell

ORVILLE SCHELL *(writer, journalist)*: For almost all of Chez Panisse's four decades of existence, my family and I have experienced it as a kind of fraternal organization. Speaking for myself, I have imagined myself some kind of a latter-day Odd Fellow who could always count on repairing to this unusual lodge hall whenever it was time to slip the surly bonds of my office and the solitude of writing, or later, the vicissitudes of academic life, for some place more convivial. There was, of course, the promise of good food, but there was also the promise of the sort of collegiality among friends—those met and as yet unmet—that created in one a sense of anticipation whenever a date for the restaurant was set. One felt that the occasion would transcend the simple act of "going out to eat."

When I became dean of the Graduate School of Journalism at UC, another whole social ecology, one that combined both public and private spaces into a new kind of fraternity, begin to elaborate itself and to envelop me and what we were doing on campus in a marvelously symbiotic way. And, the picture you see on the previous pages was one moment from this ongoing fest of the best food, enjoyable fellowship, interesting ideas, and elevating public dialogue.

The photograph shows the Dalai Lama, myself, and Richard Blum, the financier and husband to California Senator Dianne Feinstein, eating at the restaurant after one of the myriad onstage conversations that the Graduate School of Journalism organized in Zellerbach Auditorium and Wheeler Hall. In this ongoing series of events we did for the university and the Bay Area community, we broached almost every contemporary issue imaginable, from the environment and the U.S. involvement in the Middle East and the world to

the media and American politics. These events, many of which were supported by UC alumnus and philanthropist Richard Goldman, brought scores of public figures. The list included not only the Dalai Lama, but Terry Gross, Al Gore, Susan Sontag, George Soros, Robert McNamarra, Errol Morris, Bill Clinton, Tom Brokaw, Bill McKibben, Maureen Dowd, David Remnick, Sebastião Salgado, Christopher Hitchens, Christiane Amanpour, Ira Glass, Arthur Sulzberger, Peter Jennings, John Burns, Barbara Ehrenreich, Robert Silvers, Tom Friedman, and even Alice Waters.

After each event, a whole gang of us, often including the chancellor or the provost, would repair to Chez Panisse for a marvelous meal and more discussion. This combination of the public turning into the private, of the large-scale event ending in the more human-size sharing of a good meal, which was always hosted by Alice and the truly amazing Chez Panisse staff, provided a second and more intimate act to the more formal evening events. What ensued was a kind of Edible Schoolyard for the university.

Lunch with the Dalai Lama at the restaurant was just one moment in this long-running feast of good ideas and good food that over time created exactly the kind of collegium universities promise, but on which they often find it difficult to deliver. But, this one involved the campus, the community of Berkeley, and the larger world outside. The idea was to bring the world to Berkeley, and Berkeley to the world.

Of all the memorable moments during these wonderful events and meals, eating with the Dalai Lama was certainly high on the periodic table. For days, the Tibetans on the restaurant's staff were in a state of almost delirious alert and anticipation, working hard to make sure that nothing

would be amiss for their revered patriarch. Far from standing on ceremony or evincing an overly exuberant Buddhist sensitivity, His Holiness sat right down and in a very businesslike manner ordered the lamb shanks. He then ate them without apology . . .hardly surprising, given the fact that Tibetan nomads have almost nothing to eat that does not come from their yaks and sheep.

As he enjoyed this high-protein fix, he regaled us with stories of his own efforts at cooking as a child in Lhasa, recounting memories of having attempted to make some sort of Tibetan baked goods that he gleefully explained had ended up exploding in the oven!

Looking at this photo today, it is hard not to feel a certain sense of Chekhovian nostalgia, not only for that particular meal with this singular man, but also for so many other memorable meals in the always reassuringly unchanging confines of Chez Panisse. These were a truly unusual, and certainly unplanned, few years in time, when two concurrent institutions and social worlds somehow managed effortlessly to intersect to reenforce each other with a perfect yin-yang-like symbiosis. The university was the more public forum, and Chez Panisse the more private refuge, kind of a communal home situated between our public and personal lives, where we all felt welcomed. Here a public event could cool off and taper down into a more intimate conclusion.

Now, when I return to Chez Panisse, I am reminded that it is precisely this sort of space between our homes and the impersonal hurly-burly of public space that is so often missing from our new kinds of "social networks." It is this curious and welcomed role that has long made Chez Panisse more than just another restaurant at which one can get another good meal.

For His Holiness the Dalai Lama

Golden & Red beet salad
Fried Squash blossoms & lemon

Braised Lamb
with herb noodles, new garlic & Chino tomatoes
or
Goat cheese Soufflé pudding
with morels & corn

White Peach Sherbet
with gold dust peaches & berries

Chez Panisse Restaurant June 12, 1997

RUSSELL MOORE (*chef, restaurateur*): Alice asked me to be in charge of the kitchen for the meal for the Dalai Lama. The only input from the Dalai Lama's people was that he liked lamb and pasta. The only input from Alice was that she wanted the meal to be simple and beautiful and also inspiring, surprising, and divine. I really didn't think about him at first—I'm a devout atheist—I just wanted Alice to be happy. Alice and I discussed the menu, but it was her touch—golden beets in the beginning and Gold Dust peaches at the end—that created a framework for the menu.

The day of the lunch Dhondup Karpo, our farm driver and all-around hard worker, who is Tibetan, came to the restaurant, not in his trademark shorts, polo shirt, and sweater vest, but in a suit. He brought his whole family (also dressed up better than anyone in Berkeley ever does). This was my first inkling that this meal was important in a larger context, a context that was made personal to me because of my friendship with Dhondup.

We cooked lunch, the Dalai Lama ate (except the beets—he doesn't like beets?) and Dhondup and his family stood by in anticipation. After his meal the Dalai Lama came downstairs and embraced everyone in the kitchen. His embrace was disarming. I remember he hugged Cal for a particularly long time, and it was so funny to watch because Cal is twice his size. The best part was watching Dhondup be greeted by his spiritual and political leader—we were all beside ourselves. And then Dhondup thanked me for allowing him to be there and asked to take home the plates and silverware that were used by the Dalai Lama. He was weeping, I was weeping, I'm weeping now as I remember this—but I'm still an atheist who is jealous that Cal got a longer hug.

The linocut of sweet peas is by Patty Curtan; the calligraphy is by Lauren McIntosh. We were told that the Dalai Lama would eat compassionately raised animals, but not that he was forbidden to eat anything that grew underground.

Dinner for the President

Fresh anchovies and green olive tapenade toasts
grilled artichoke hearts and squash blossom fritters

Bodega Bay King Salmon
with Meyer lemon vinaigrette

Lulu Peyraud's soupe au pistou
with summer vegetables and lamb

Garden salad

Wild blackberries and baked stuffed peaches

July 23, 1996 at the home of Susie Tompkins, San Francisco

I was sure if I fed the president a perfect peach—the most delicious food—it would bring him to a new understanding of the politics of food. But we had no peaches when he came to the restaurant in 1993, so he got a Gravenstein apple. He loved it, but I saw him eyeing the boysenberry ice cream on another table. Three years later, at a fundraiser, we fed him the menu on the opposite page.

GREIL MARCUS (*music critic, historian, and director, Pagnol et Cie., Inc.*): This night at Chez Panisse in 1993 was a chance to show Bill Clinton what real food tasted like, in small portions, so that each bite could be looked at, considered, tasted, so you, as an eater, could enter that conversation with what you ate. So at Clinton's table there were small orange tomatoes, fettuccine with crab and corn, green beans and chanterelles, a pizza, homemade prosciutto, raspberries, strawberries, apples, and a lemon custard tart, as much a signature dish as any Chez Panisse has ever devised.

But it was not merely a chance to show what the restaurant could do; it was a chance to speak to a president, a president you had voted for, someone in whom you had already invested your own hopes, and tell him what ought to be done about the nation's health, its food supply, why what people ate would shape their future and that of the country itself. It wasn't only Alice who felt that way, who pressed Clinton on the message it would send, the glow that would radiate, if there were an organic garden at the White House.

A Sun Crest peach from Frog Hollow Farm, Brentwood, California.

169

our first ladies

Lunch for
First Lady Hillary Rodham Clinton
and Tipper Gore
❧
Women's Leadership Forum

Hors d'oeuvre in the kitchen

Soup of fresh fava beans and peas
from our Berkeley garden

Bodega Bay salmon with new potatoes,
red lettuces and white asparagus salad

The Chinos' Mara des Bois strawberry sherbet
with rose granita

Edible Schoolyard lemon verbena tisane

Chez Panisse   12 June 1999

Hillary Rodham Clinton

My friend Susie Buell, pictured above with Hillary Clinton, was the first person to give money to the Edible Schoolyard, and her passion for social justice strongly influenced the development of the project. Susie champions charismatic and eloquent speakers, leaders who can deliver messages for us in ways we never could ourselves. I never imagined she would bring Hillary Clinton and Tipper Gore to Chez Panisse. It was such a gift. We wanted desperately to live up to their expectations of us. I remember talking earnestly to Hillary about planting a garden at the White House. And I was delighted to hear later that they planted a vegetable garden on the roof.

SUSIE TOMPKINS BUELL *(philanthropist, activist)*: When you take people to Chez Panisse you can be sure it will awaken their senses. Of course whoever goes there will learn something about food, but it touches you in other ways, too. All your senses are touched. There's the clang of the pots and the look of the light and the smells coming out of the kitchen and the feel of the air. And the talk across the table. You're sitting there, and suddenly, you realize how alive you are. It's so exciting. It just touches you. Chez Panisse validates the sensual in so many ways.

If you think about it, the people with the most responsibility in the world need to be sensualists. People who are sensualists feel their humanity. It's what's missing in politics. Politicians live in a bubble. They need to get out in nature and experience beauty around them. I've done a lot of fund-raisers. This one at Chez Panisse was for Hillary Clinton when she was running for the Senate. Tipper Gore was there, and it was great because it was one of the last times that the two of them were together like that: the outgoing first lady with the possibly incoming first lady. We know what happened there. But at the time, it was so exciting. There was an electricity in the air because of all the possibility.

My generation is the way it is because we grew up in the sixties. We had this feeling we could change the world. And those of us who were lucky enough to travel wanted to bring back our experiences of people in other countries and share them with the people back home. Some of us have been able to do that through our businesses and our careers and lives. And we're still trying. The sixties are so much a part of the food culture, whether anyone realizes it or not. We're still being inspired by the sixties—by the feeling of unlimited possibilities.

In a way, Julia Child was the mother of us all. It's hard to believe that Chez Panisse would ever have opened without her trailblazing effect on American taste. Her television show had been running for eight years when we started the restaurant, and thanks to her, millions of viewers had begun to think of food in a different way. She visited Chez Panisse several times with her husband, Paul. They were so devoted to each other. Later, when he was unable to travel and she had to come without him, she always telephoned to make sure he was all right.

MENU FOR JULIA CHILD

Watercress salad with green garlic

Baked whole fish with fennel oil

Garbure with goose confit cooked in the hearth

Blood orange sherbet and fruit compote

Château La Louvière *from Jean-Pierre & Denise*
With affection from Chez Panisse
February 25, 1993

I use this phrase all the time: *la famille Panisse*. The Panisse family. And it really is a family, an extended, living, breathing family. Somehow, almost without knowing it, a network of people has woven itself together, connecting for life, like it or not. Chez Panisse has become a real home, in the deepest sense. It has become the place where, as Robert Frost says, when you have to go there, they have to take you in. And it is a dynamic family, always adding new members, always in flux, probably never completely sure where its boundaries really are. What I do know is that we have come to constitute a circle of friends who can count on one another above and beyond the exigencies of running the actual restaurant. In my self-absorbed way, I sometimes think of myself as filling the role of the dictatorial matriarch. But in all likelihood, that is a delusion. There is a larger, more inclusive, more modest spirit at work here: the spirit of Panisse—kindly, devoted, benevolent, happy at work, looking to the future.

la famille Panisse

FROM LEFT:
David Stewart,
Steve Crumley,
Patty Curtan,
Alice, Alan Tangren,
Jean-Pierre Moullé,
Lindsey Shere,
Fritz Streiff,
Charles Shere

Jean-Pierre Moullé, downstairs chef, prepares scallops for the dining room with Jérôme Waag and Philip Dedlow, circa 2002.

30

Chez Panisse

a long

lunch outdoors

Iowa, 1912

When I was starting to worry about what we would do for a thirtieth birthday party to celebrate and to raise money for the foundation, I found this picture in a book of early twentieth-century postcards. I thought, oh my goodness. It's a picture of exactly the celebration we need to produce: a big crowd, in their Sunday best, seated at long tables under a canopy of trees for a summer banquet outdoors. But how do we get there? It took a year of planning. We sent out an invitation that promised a vision of lambs turning slowly on spits as aromatic smoke wreathed the base of the campanile (which you were invited to ascend); an exhibition of restaurant art, posters, and menus for special occasions; and a sparkling apéritif and *panisses* (the fried chickpea-flour street food of Nice); and, once the guests were summoned to table, a long lunch that would fade imperceptibly into dinner and culminate with staged entertainments and sentimental toasts. Then we had to figure out how to deliver on our promises.

GRANDE FÊTE CHAMPÊTRE

A LONG LUNCH OUTDOORS CELEBRATING

CHEZ PANISSE

on its Thirtieth Birthday

at the University of California, Berkeley

on the Campanile Esplanade

Sunday, August 26, 2001

ONE P.M. UNTIL TWILIGHT

A benefit for the Chez Panisse Foundation

déjeuner sur l'herbe
AUGUST 28, 2001, BERKELEY

NICHOLAS MCGEGAN (conductor; music director, Philharmonia Baroque Orchestra): All of us have been to many parties in our lives: some dull parties, some good parties—some wild parties, even. But we can count on the fingers of one hand the truly great parties, those where time seems to stop and years afterward we can remember things as if they happened yesterday. The party to celebrate the thirtieth anniversary of Chez Panisse was the very best of the best. Bacchus and the other gods of jollity conspired, on a beautiful August afternoon, to give us all a slice of the kind of life they are supposed to enjoy for eternity. We did much better than mere ambrosia, too. The delicious charcuterie and Provençal lamb would surely have made the jaded Olympians jealous. My tiny part was to provide some horn fanfares to summon everyone to dinner. Good music and good food are natural soul mates: not the prepackaged music that restaurateurs (misguidedly) seem to think increases our pleasure while we eat; but brief, festive live music that didn't stifle conversation but simply heightened the sense of occasion and whetted our sensory appetite.

I and my partner, David, were thrilled to be at a table that was a real Bay Area *café des artistes*. The conversation was as great as the food and the wine. It was a modern-day *déjeuner sur l'herbe*; the very finest kind of picnic. Afterward came the entertainment. I especially remember Mark Morris's vocal performance and Dario Cecchini's recital of Dante. As Horace, no stranger to a good party, wrote two thousand years ago, "Lord, send me more such afternoons as this."

tout le monde à table!

CAROLYN FEDERMAN (*event director, former development director, Chez Panisse Foundation*): The thirtieth birthday celebration of Chez Panisse was originally conceived as a picnic under the trees for a hundred and fifty or so friends of the restaurant. In true Chez Panisse style, the event grew organically to involve over six hundred guests at a day-long meal; over two hundred past and current chefs from Chez Panisse; two hundred volunteers from all over the country; four octegenarian chefs to be celebrated for their contribution to the culinary world; and a host of fans, regulars, and celebrity guests come to raise a toast to thirty years of their favorite place to eat.

When I first met Alice to discuss planning and coordinating the event, I didn't know anything about her. I had heard of Chez Panisse: it was one of those nice restaurants you went to when you graduated. I had eaten there once. As we talked, she quietly—meekly, even—began to draw a picture of the event she envisioned: a ridiculously complex production with thousands of moving parts. An outdoor theater, dozens of fifteen-foot tables decorated by hand, visitors from all over the world performing food theater in a staged market; Michael Tilson Thomas playing piano; Mark Morris dancing the menu; Julia Child, Edna Lewis, Cecilia Chiang, Lulu Peyraud, and Marion Cunningham honored on a hand-painted stage; two hundred lambs roasting on spits. More. Impossible! I left that first meeting thinking, This woman is absolutely mad. Over time, I came to understand that she would have everything she wanted; and that the dedicated family of Chez Panisse would go to unbelievable lengths to make each and every detail not just perfect but brilliant, and unfathomably delicious.

As two hundred Chez Panisse chefs, past and present, descended on Berkeley to lend their support, and two hundred regulars, fans, and acolytes volunteered for various roles, I got a crash course in the entire history of the restaurant and its profound influence on the culinary world. I came to meet nearly every single individual who had ever been involved with the restaurant in any capacity. At countless committee meetings to discuss yellow jackets, décor, chefs, entertainment, film, and on and on, I got to know the extended family of Panisse. What struck me most about the whole experience was how each person rose to meet Alice's uncompromising expectations.

Alice changed the menu that very morning, based on what looked best in the market, and the entire crew, from chef to server to runner, adjusted accordingly, without blinking an eye. Everything was perfect. Guests milled about a little bit, but for the most part they spent the entire day seated at the long tables, laughing, eating, and celebrating the family and culture of Chez Panisse.

The Chez Panisse family created new recipes, new art, found a way around every problem, never said no, and simply made it all happen in the most elegant and astonishing way. I have never before or since met such an extraordinary collection of people. Their talent, humor, and generosity swept me up like an August breeze. It was positively euphoric to be part of their world.

COLMAN ANDREWS (*writer*): In a way, that "long lunch" in the shadow of the UC campanile made up for all the meals I had to miss for various reasons at the restaurant over the years. There were so many people there, scores of old friends to reconnect with, new friends to make, two or three old lovers, probably an enemy or two, celebrities of every stripe, chefs from every era— and that beautiful day and the smells in the air and those sardines, that lamb, the warm *panisses,* the fish soup good enough to drown in.

It was a long lunch for a reason: I wanted it to be the best of all possible parties—and something more: a gathering where all sorts of people who had never met before—busboys and bankers, politicians and artists, professors and farmers—would suddenly make unexpected, unlikely, exciting connections; where conversation would slow down and broaden; and where, for one afternoon, a vision of a fulfilling future, where all your senses were fully engaged, was made undeniably, unforgettably real.

SCOTT PEACOCK (*chef, writer*): It was almost surreal how large it was. It hardly seemed possible that such a big crowd had gathered. I mean, it felt like the whole town of Berkeley was there in some kind of village square. I felt a kind of tingly excitement. It was such a privilege to be there. Of course everywhere you looked there were people like George Lucas or Martha Stewart, but the thing that excited me the most was that despite the vast scale of the whole thing, it felt intimate. It was done in that typical Chez Panisse way, where even though the event was humongous on one level, everything and everyone was attended to in such a simple, beautiful, and fine way. Even though the party involved a thousand people, the food came out beautifully and effortlessly, and you didn't feel like you were in a crowd. You felt taken care of.

I was escorting Edna Lewis, one of the honorees. She loved it. We got there the day before the birthday and wanted to go to the restaurant to say hi, but we knew people would be busy: they were serving dinner and getting ready for the party. We went anyway. People were spilling out onto Shattuck Avenue. Alice was completely crazed. She told us they were completely booked—but they could set up a little table in the kitchen. So we sat at that table while Alice was running around, putting boxes of radishes in the walk-in, and there was no end to the comings and goings. I remember we were eating olives, but someone forgot to give us a plate for the pits, so there was a pile of pits on the table—mostly from me, I'm sure—and Alice came by and picked up the pits amidst all this craziness, and it was so great. It made me feel like we were the only people in the world that mattered. I'm sure Miss Lewis felt that way, too.

Another thing I remember about being so well taken care of at the thirtieth was that Alice had appointed ambassadors to make sure people from out of town were OK. Davia Nelson, Margaret Grade, Sue Murphy, and Cristina Salas-Porras were among them. Margaret was wearing a hat that was like an ultrachic hybrid of a nurse's cap and the flying nun's wimple. Cristina fed us those mulberry ice cream cones, and I'm sure I ate too many.

MENU

RECEPTION AT THE CAMPANILE
Dario Cecchini's pork specialties from Panzano
Panisses, radishes, and almonds

LUNCH À LA FAMILLE ON THE ESPLANADE
Summer vegetable salads

Provençal fish soup cooked in the fireplace

Spit-roasted barons of Canfield Farm lamb with chanterelles
Spicy lamb and mint sausages
Fresh shell beans
Herb salad

Cheese from Jean d'Alos
Apple and plum jellies

Mulberry ice cream cones
Friandises and tisane

WINES DONATED BY KERMIT LYNCH WINE MERCHANT
Prosecco Brut *Bosco di Gica*, Adriano Adami
2000 Bandol Rosé, Domaine Tempier
1999 Bourgogne Blanc, Côte Chalonnaise *Les Clous*, A & P De Villaine
1999 Gigondas, Domaine les Pallières
1999 Muscat de Beaumes-de-Venise, Domaine de Durban

Menu Prepared by the Chefs and Friends of Chez Panisse
with Ingredients Produced by Local Organic Farms and Ranches

26 AUGUST 2001

CHEZ PANISSE THIRTIETH BIRTHDAY

The night before the event a group of us gathered around the oval table in my kitchen next to the fire in the hearth, agonizing over the seating chart. Who should sit next to whom? Who should be separated? I kept trying to fine-tune it and couldn't let go until the others were ready to throw me in the fire. Now I wish I hadn't tortured myself about it so much. When the time came, people found the way to where they were supposed to be.

SUE MURPHY *(comic, writer, producer)*: Alice and I got there very early, and it was a beautiful morning. Sometimes it can be foggy and cold early in the day in Berkeley in August, but this morning the sun was shining. It seemed like Alice was everywhere, saying, "Put those glasses over there! Make sure that table is level!" I would see her in one place, and then a second later in a completely different place.

I remember looking across the campanile esplanade and seeing activity in every corner. There were bars being set up, and grills and tables, and busing stations, and you would jump in anywhere that needed help while the little chef that could was darting about, making sure every detail was the way it should be.

There was a focused energy on the task at hand, but everyone was happy and laughing and greeting friends and people they hadn't worked with or seen in a while. With everyone's help it all came together: the sea of tables was set, the stage was covered with flowers, and the smell of the fires in the grills wafted over the plaza. It was pretty fantastic.

All the chefs and the waitstaff got together and Alice gave them her St. Crispin's Day speech. She basically said, be brilliant, work hard, make it beautiful like you all know how to do, but don't forget to celebrate.

I was terrified there would be yellow jacket wasps hovering over the food and stinging the guests, because that had been a problem when I attended a graduation event at the site earlier that summer. So I invited entomologists from the university to have lunch at the Café and advise us. To my delight, they volunteered to wrangle all the yellow jacket nests on campus and move them a mile uphill from the party site a few days before. I don't know how they did it, but when the day came, no wasps crashed the party.

FAITH WILLINGER *(maestra)*: I am Dario Cecchini's sister. Dario (*above*) is the world's greatest butcher. We went to the Chez Panisse birthday together. I translated. We did a *sopressata* (head cheese) demonstration for chefs and aspiring salumi makers. We brought Alice a bouquet of wild fennel greens and flowers, picked in the parking lot. The campanile tolled. Dario responded by reciting Canto V of Dante's *Inferno* (the story of Paolo and Francesca). Knowledge of Dante's Tuscan Italian, which flows through Dario's veins, was unnecessary.

Everyone was working so hard and cooking, but right before the lambs got spitted, someone said you need to get everyone together to take a picture. We posed for the picture (*left*), but there were many who couldn't leave their posts, so it's really not complete. It was such an extraordinary thing to see this kind of beautiful assembly, with everyone together like this. It was a cooks' reunion, with restaurateurs and caterers and private chefs and food purveyors.

a charming little stage

Among those gracing Jude Fletcher and Dave Brandon's inspired hand-painted stage of a bucolic Northern Californian landscape were Ruth Reichl, Edna Lewis, Johnny Apple, Michael Tilson Thomas, Greil Marcus, Senator Barbara Boxer, and my parents.

BETSEY APPLE *(wife of journalist Johnny Apple)*: For well over a quarter of a century, as Johnny and I zigzagged across the world for work and play, we always headed to Shattuck Avenue when landing on the West Coast. We couldn't resist Chez Panisse's siren call. In the early days we had countless sensational lunches with our friends Charles and Doris, the marvelous Muscatines, tasting the simplest and best ingredients imaginable to man. And then the timeline begins to blur—so many other hedonistic visits, eating both up and downstairs, celebrating anything we could think of, just so long as we could be in the hands of that fantastic cooking crew.

At the birthday blowout on the Berkeley campus, Johnny was one of the speakers. On that bright sunny day, he lauded the wonderful new world created by his friend and her happy band. Several years later at Johnny's memorial service, Alice spoke glowingly about Johnny's writing and his contribution to this new world of food. It was deeply touching.

A lovely, loving friendship. How much Chez Panisse has given us all.

"Let's have another cup of coffee, and let's have another piece of pie." Irving Berlin

It's all a blur to me now. Michael Tilson Thomas had composed a marching song for the occasion, and that was sung earlier, with Michael at the piano. And then there were speeches and toasts. But I didn't know Mark Morris was going to sing. I thought he was going to dance! And all of a sudden, there he was at the microphone, an accompanist sat down at the piano, and Mark launched into Irving Berlin's "Let's Have Another Cup of Coffee." Somebody had cued the dessert chefs to march on with birthday cakes with burning candles on them when Mark took the stage, and they stood there, holding their flaming cakes as he sang. The trouble was, he observed the repeat in the score and sang the whole song twice, so the birthday candles had started guttering, melting, and drip-ping and the dessert chefs had to stand there, worrying whether he would finish before the cakes were ruined.

PATRICK MARTINS (*cofounder, Heritage Foods USA*): My role was to entertain the guests who were driven in a van because they were too frail to walk from the parking lot to the event space on the campus. To prepare I rented the movie *Speed* so I would be ready for anything, even a bomb detonating if the van's velocity fell below sixty miles per hour. That day I scaled comedic heights even the greatest comics would envy; I've never been funnier. Chez Panisse inspires people!

GILBERT PILGRAM (*owner, Zuni Café; former general manager, Chez Panisse*): I was always in charge of cleaning up. When we started having meetings to plan the birthday, about a year in advance, at the end of every meeting I would say, "OK, so can we talk about cleanup?" and Alice would say, "Gilbert, don't worry about it, we've got it taken care of, you won't have to do it this time." And then the next meeting would come and I would say, "I just want to make sure the cleanup is covered," and Alice finally said, "Gilbert, if I have to hear another thing about cleanup, I'm going to go crazy. It's taken care of!"

The day of the event, Briar Brown, Steve Jobs's chef, who used to work at the restaurant, said, "Gilbert, you have a huge problem. How are you going to clean up? The logic is all wrong. Everything came packed tightly in two trucks, but now everyone is taking everything all over the place, no one's paying attention, and you're never going to fit it all back into the trucks." I said, "I don't need to worry, Alice says it's taken care of." At the end of the night everyone left but me, Carolyn and her husband, and a friend of Cristina's. No cleaning crew in sight, and everyone who had worked was at the afterparty — where they had a mariachi band and no one was picking up the phone, because they couldn't hear it. We were all alone until we saw a band of Tibetans arrive. So it was just us and a few middle-aged Tibetan women and seven or eight teenagers who didn't want to be there. It took us until sunrise to clean up the site.

Above is one of the giant decorated loaves of levain bread baked for the party by Steve Sullivan's Acme Bread Company. Marcel Pagnol's other great movie, *The Baker's Wife,* taught me an unforgettable lesson: as marriage is to individuals, so is good bread to the daily life of a community. Nothing communicates health, unity, and redemption better than good bread.

attention to detail

As I approached the thirtieth birthday, I began to think that it was important to have a document that described who we were and how we lived. I asked my friend Bob Carrau to take some pictures, because I knew he had a good eye and an inquisitive disposition. He took pleasure in exploring the little corners of the operation where people were enjoying their daily routines and quietly attending to the beautiful details: cutting pasta, plucking leaves, boning fowl, shelling peas, washing dishes, folding napkins—all the careful, precise work that makes the food taste good and the place feel homelike. It's work that can't be done on autopilot; it has to be done with intention—and passion. The pictures prove that. Bob says he always thinks of these photos as stills from a movie that never got made.

plus ça change...

After almost twenty years, the Café deserved a cookbook of its own. In its third decade, the Café grew ever stronger, more savory, and more self-reliant—although it still had plenty of quirks of its own. David Tanis was the perfect cook to write a Café cookbook: he had been one of the chefs of the Café kitchen during its adolescence, and his honest, soulful food was right at the core of the Café's identity. I invited David Goines to design and illustrate, which he did, as always, inimitably. Three of the photos at left show David Tanis at work writing the menu, peeling apples, and in the downstairs kitchen. The smiling waiter with the goatee is Martin Johnson, now also a maître d'hôtel. In the bottom row, from left, are John Chalik and Tim Savinar, both of whom have served as chairman of our board of directors; Patty Unterman, the food writer and restaurateur; David King, scientist and scholar, with Alta Tingle, another of our directors; and Stephanie Sugawara, a former waiter, with Jonathan Waters, maître d'hôtel and current director of our wine cellar.

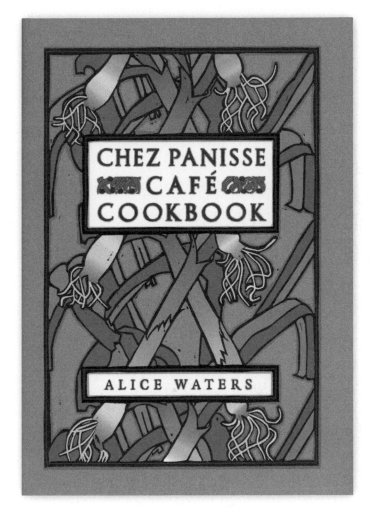

CHEZ PANISSE CAFÉ COOKBOOK

ALICE WATERS

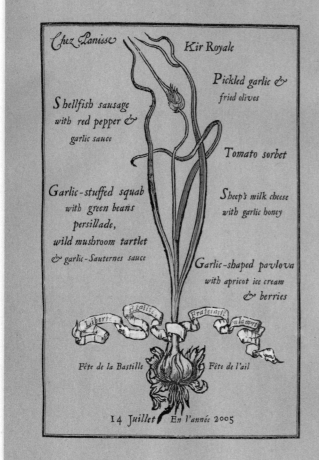

In 1975, one of our customers, John Harris, the author of a book about garlic and the self-styled "head garlic-head" behind the Lovers of the Stinking Rose, suggested that we celebrate the California garlic harvest. Since the harvest usually falls close to Bastille Day, he proposed a garlic festival on the French national holiday, which we would of course be observing anyway. Thus began an annual estival festival tradition: the Gallic garlic gala, in which there's an alliaceous element to every Provençal-inspired course. It's an excuse to hire a band or two: in the early days, a Cajun band led by Danny Poullard; more recently, Odile Lavault and the Baguette Quartette, who play ineffably French acoustic *bal musette* music, complete with whirling virtuoso accordion riffs. Last year, late at night, when Odile and her band finished their last set, they were replaced by a jazz combo led by our busboy Rafael Postel. Usually, at some point in the evening, "La Marseillaise" is sung.

liberté, égalité, fraternité!

BASTILLE DAY GARLIC FESTIVAL

Chez P...

MENU for

200...

Happy Ne...

from Alice, Fa...

the family of...

...nisse

PEACE

...r Year

...ny, and

...Panisse

During the run-up to
the invasion of Iraq,
and even more so in
its aftermath, antiwar
sentiment once again
became mainstream,
at least in Berkeley.
Although it may be
ineffectual and even
slightly self-indulgent for
the Chez Panisse family
to declare ourselves
repeatedly for peace,
we can't help it.

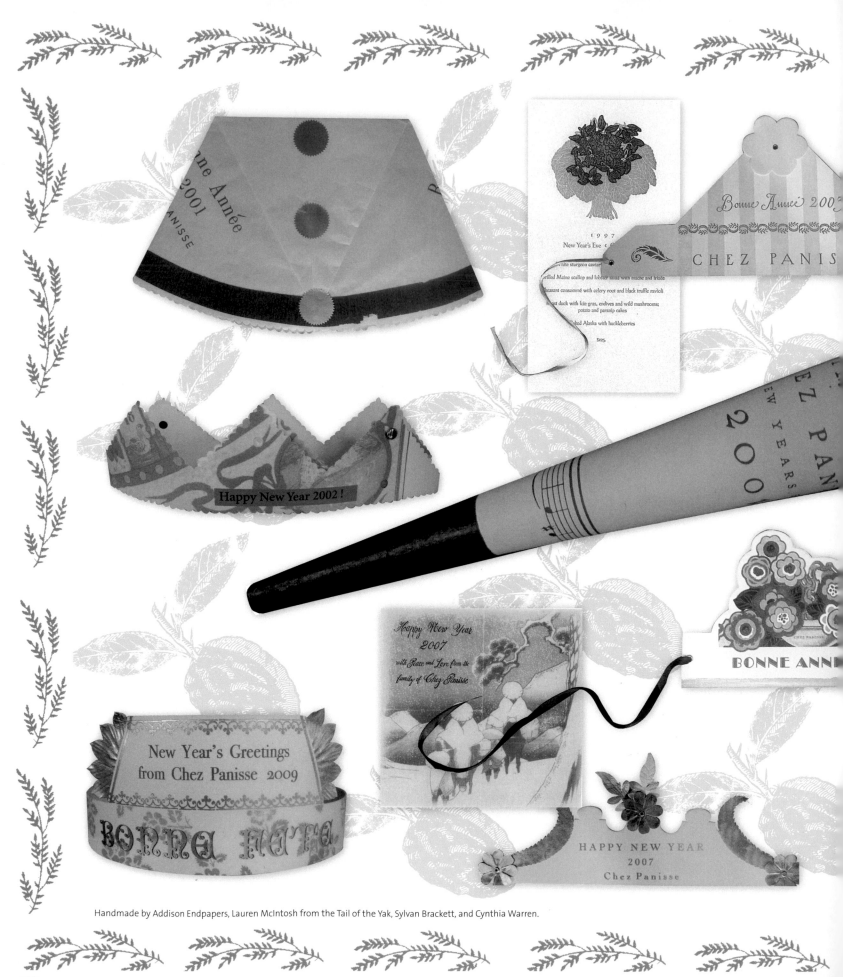

ne Année
2001
ANISSE

1997
New Year's Eve

hite sturgeon caviar
grilled Maine scallop and lobster salad with mache and frisée
pheasant consommé with celery root and black truffle ravioli
roast duck with foie gras, endives and wild mushrooms;
potato and parsnip cakes
baked Alaska with huckleberries

$125.

Bonne Année 2003

CHEZ PANISSE

Happy New Year 2002 !

EZ PAN
EW YEARS
2 0 0

Happy New Year
2007
with Peace and Love from the
family of Chez Panisse

BONNE ANN

New Year's Greetings
from Chez Panisse 2009

Bonna nova

HAPPY NEW YEAR
2007
Chez Panisse

Handmade by Addison Endpapers, Lauren McIntosh from the Tail of the Yak, Sylvan Brackett, and Cynthia Warren.

souvenirs
de la fête

a sustainable prince

I had met the Prince of Wales with Eric Schlosser in London, and admired him for his tireless support of organic farming. Has any other high-profile world figure done as much to promote the values of sustainability? His visit to California in 2005 included a formal dinner in his honor arranged by the British consul-general and by Stanlee Gatti, who is San Francisco's preeminent stager of gala events. I jumped at the invitation to put together a team of cooks and waiters. Best of all, the prince and the Duchess of Cornwall agreed to visit The Edible Schoolyard and the farmers' market in Point Reyes.

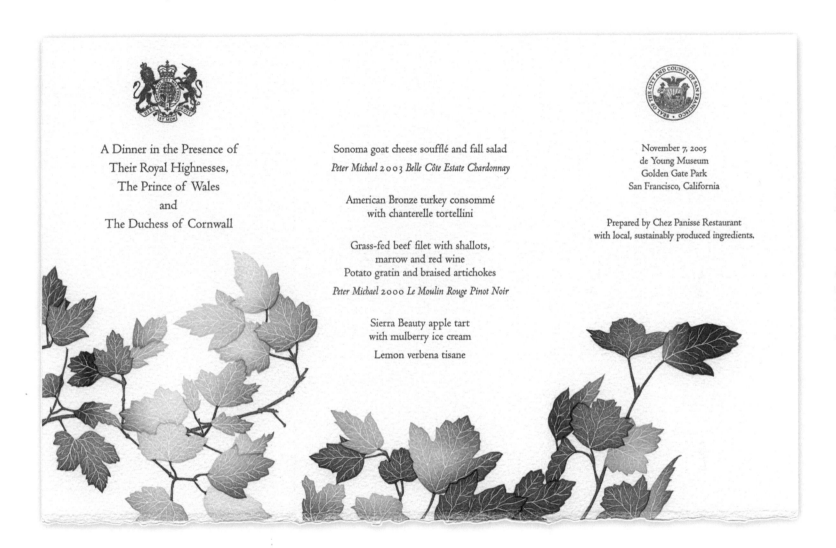

A Dinner in the Presence of
Their Royal Highnesses,
The Prince of Wales
and
The Duchess of Cornwall

Sonoma goat cheese soufflé and fall salad
Peter Michael 2003 Belle Côte Estate Chardonnay

American Bronze turkey consommé
with chanterelle tortellini

Grass-fed beef filet with shallots,
marrow and red wine
Potato gratin and braised artichokes
Peter Michael 2000 Le Moulin Rouge Pinot Noir

Sierra Beauty apple tart
with mulberry ice cream
Lemon verbena tisane

November 7, 2005
de Young Museum
Golden Gate Park
San Francisco, California

Prepared by Chez Panisse Restaurant
with local, sustainably produced ingredients.

GILBERT PILGRAM *(chef, owner, Zuni Café; former general manager, Chez Panisse)*: The dinner we catered for the Prince of Wales and his consort went very well. It was held at the brand-new de Young Museum in a room lined with beautiful murals of Northern California. We borrowed plates from Heath, handblown glasses from Simon Pearce in Vermont, and a very valuable collection of Georgian silver flatware. I was more nervous about losing the silverware than I was about meeting the prince. There were three different sets, and I had to make sure that no one walked away with any. Everyone in the prince's entourage and everyone from the British consul-general's staff was incredibly gracious. The secretary to the British ambassador took a liking to me and let me announce the guests, just like in the movies. The door would open, and in my best basso profundo voice I had to declaim whatever it is the majordomo is supposed to declaim, with all the proper titles and honorifics, "Lord So-and-so of So-and-so and Lady So-and-so," and I would escort them to their seats. The Duchess of Cornwall took my arm, and I led her to her chair across the table from the prince. She was very pleasant. I observed that she was eating her salad with her hands, and because I was so nervous about the silverware my first thought was, where's the silver? But at the end of the night, every fork, knife, and spoon was accounted for.

collaborating with artists

Ann Hamilton's installation (*opposite*) at the Capp Street Project, an experimental art space in San Francisco, had a visceral impact on me: live sheep, a carpet of pennies overlapping like fish scales on a bed of oozing honey. Here was an artist I had to collaborate with. And I did, with dinners at the Whitney Museum and, as a benefit for the Chez Panisse Foundation, at the sculpture garden of Steve Oliver (*top, flanked by me and Ann*) at his Sonoma ranch, where Ann built an extraordinary tower.

ANN HAMILTON (*artist*):

making

the smell of animals before the sight / at the back of the space / three sheep living under a skylight on a bed of green alfalfa / facing you and an undulating floor of copper / pennies / a landscape of them / hand laid / a giant rectangle on the floor / a gathering together / perhaps a little loud, a little garish / perhaps related to one of Liberace's jackets / a copper carpet / a perfect rectangle / leaching honey at its edges / privation and excess / each act of hand / transparently present / in the drifts and eddies that pattern the coins / the product of a human economy laid into the sweet sticky substance of an animal one / a mutuality of dependence / nature dependent on human nurture / human nurture dependent on nature / a gaze exchanged across silent language / touching our animal selves / face to face / across species

imagination comes from animal bodies / words come from bodies /we make with words

across the table / face to face /eating and listening and speaking and working / acts of attention and recognition / born in smelling and feeling and tasting and sharing and touching and seeing and loving and talking and arguing and making up /
the first horizon / our sociability / a glance exchanged/ a recognition / my blank page /

where up down / right hand left hand / inside outside / sky ground / meet and all things seem possible / face to face /
at table

the coat that keeps you warm

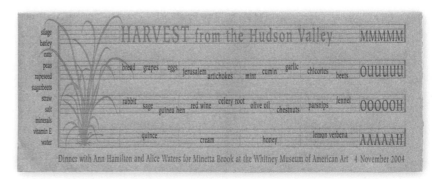

HARVEST from the Hudson Valley

silage, barley, oats, peas, rapeseed, sugarbeets, straw, salt, minerals, vitamin E, water

bread, grapes, eggs, jerusalem artichokes, mint, cumin, garlic, chicories, beets

rabbit, sage, guinea hen, red wine, celery root, olive oil, chestnuts, parsnips, fennel

quince, cream, honey, lemon verbena

MMMMM / OUUUUU / OOOOOH / AAAAAH

Dinner with Ann Hamilton and Alice Waters for Minetta Brook at the Whitney Museum of American Art 4 November 2004

Dinner with Mikhail Baryshnikov, Alice Waters and Robert Cole

Platters of shellfish and salads à la Panisse

Borage ravioli

Filet of beef Baryshnikov

Apricot soufflé

Thank you so kindly . . .

Misha

A Benefit for the Baryshnikov Art Center, New York and Cal Performances, UC Berkeley

19 June 2003   Chez Panisse

Mikhail Baryshnikov came to Chez Panisse for the first time after a performance, late; I liked him so much I waived our no-smoking rule and let him smoke a cigar. Years later, the Sundance Channel made a documentary series called *Iconoclasts*, the point of which was to stage collaborations between people who were accomplished in ostensibly unconnected disciplines. Of the partners proposed, Misha was my first choice. I knew our fields were somehow related, and I knew he would love The Edible Schoolyard because he's a teacher, too.

CRISTINA SALAS-PORRAS *(former assistant to Alice)*: Mikhail Baryshnikov has an appreciation of food that's a little like Alice's appreciation of dance. They both know each other's field is deep, but they don't quite know just how deep. Of course, Alice wanted him to improve the food at his dancing school in New York, so she sent me there with a little picnic lunch for him. It was a sort of Irish bento box: there was soup, some smoked salmon, soda bread, and little pickles. When he was out of his office I set the table with beautiful napkins and nice plates, and I set things out so he had little options to eat. A friend of mine knew an old Russian proverb that means something like "you are what you eat," and I printed that out in Russian and put it on the table. He got the message.

Mikhail Baryshnikov,
Fanny Singer, and
Alice share lunch
with dance students
in New York.

As a friend of creative collaboration, and because I had been so deeply affected by the seriousness and timeliness of the opera *Doctor Atomic*, I felt compelled to host an event for the artists who had put together its world premiere at the San Francisco Opera. John Adams has been a resident of Berkeley for years, and Peter Sellars has become one of my most beloved sources of inspiration and encouragement.

CLOCKWISE FROM TOP LEFT: John Adams; scenes from the Lyric Opera of Chicago production (coproduced by the San Francisco Opera and the Netherlands Opera) with Gerald Finley and Jessica Rivera.

singing and bringing it forth

DOCTOR ATOMIC, AN OPERA BY JOHN ADAMS AND PETER SELLARS

JOHN ADAMS *(composer)*: *Doctor Atomic* is an opera about the great physicist J. Robert Oppenheimer and the creation of the first atomic bomb. Oppenheimer and many of the other scientists who worked with him at Los Alamos were Berkeley people. "Oppie," a charismatic young professor at UC when he was picked by the army to spearhead the Manhattan Project, was a highly cultivated man who loved literature, art, classical music, and good food. In those menu-impoverished days his restaurant of choice to entertain friends was the old Trader Vic's in San Francisco. What a pity Chez Panisse didn't exist back then! If it did, there's no question in my mind that Oppie would have been a CP regular (although something would have to be done about his chain-smoking!).

Putting on a world premiere of a three-hour opera means many months of intense work and sustained effort from the singers, the musical and theatrical staff, and all those who labor to bring such a complex piece to light. It's a tremendously emotional experience—hundreds if not thousands of hours of fiendishly difficult work all leading up to the anxiety and jitters of opening night. In the world of opera anything can go wrong and usually does. Fortunately, the San Francisco Opera came through and delivered a memorable production, the kind most composers never live to see.

Shortly after the premiere, Alice, with her customary generosity and vivacity, welcomed the cast of *Doctor Atomic* with a special dinner to commemorate the event. It was an opportunity to unwind, to laugh, tell stories, and just have a really good time. Everyone felt privileged to be so honored, and I know that the event spoke of the whole artistic community's deep gratitude to these very talented performers.

Who knows how many creative projects have been hatched over a lunch or late night dinner at the restaurant? In the nearly thirty years that I've lived in Berkeley I've had many a "huddle" at Chez Panisse with composers, conductors, choreographers, producers—all the time keeping an eye on the artistry going on in the kitchen or at the pizza oven. It's a tradition—part of the good life that we are so fortunate to be able to share.

PETER SELLARS *(director)*: The birth of a major new opera is always an overwhelming experience. Two weeks after the opening, we were still trying to understand what we had brought into the world. Alice Waters gave us a chance to catch our breath and reflect in an atmosphere of warmth, friends, and extremely beautiful food. I will never forget my first visit to Chez Panisse—coming up the stairs I met the bartender Robert Messick, who had flown to the Salzburg Festival the previous year to see my production of Messiaen's six-hour transcendent mega-opera, *Saint-François d'Assise*. I caught my breath—these are the kind of people who are serving and cooking for us.

MENU for PETER & JOHN & Friends of Doctor Atomic

Chez Panisse Restaurant
October 9, 2005

Prosecco with pomegranate
Roasted cashews, pickles, olives,
fresh anchovy toasts, stuffed eggs

❁

Fresh corn tamal with roasted peppers,
tomatoes, and chanterelles

❁

Spit-roasted Cattail Creek Ranch lamb
with shell beans, fried eggplant,
and garden salad

❁

Plum tart with raspberry ice cream

take your time

FANNY SINGER (student, writer): Though I saw many extraordinary artworks in various states of completion throughout Olafur's studio, from lamps shaped like crystals to a film made up of colorful geometric forms, I was most impressed by the long table and the beautiful adjacent kitchen where his cooks prepare meals for the fabricators, architects, artists, and writers who populate the many floors of his colossal studio.

Olafur's art, which at first glance can seem cold and modern, seeks to engage the viewer universally. Seeing his art is like sitting down to a meal: a necessary human function, but one of tremendous sensuous possibility that makes you feel viscerally connected to something outside yourself. Olafur has embraced the humanness of viewing art, reclaiming it from the realm of pure, uninvolved spectacle. In many cases, his art requires that our bodies transform the art itself; but the art, whether it is a meal or a huge sun installed in the London Tate's Turbine Hall, has the potential to change both our bodies and our thinking.

When I first met the artist Olafur Eliasson not long after his Tate Modern installation (*opposite*), we realized that we share a passion not just for food, but for the conviviality of the table. When he told me about the imminent opening of his show "Take Your Time" at the Chicago Museum of Contemporary Art, I proposed that Chez Panisse create a meal for the occasion. I wanted the dinner to reflect some of the things that Olafur's art expresses so clearly: an emphasis on the senses and on the slowing down of time that's necessary in order to truly understand something sensuously. We set up a single table (*left*) and my artist and designer friend Christina Kim adorned it with a hand-sewn tablecloth and napkins silkscreened with shapes recalling Olafur's experiments in sculpture and architecture. Patty Curtan printed the menu, highlighting each vegetable in a green that suggested the beginning of spring. Later, I visited Olafur's studio in Berlin. The first room I entered was a great hall dominated by a long dining table. There, beneath a clerestory that admits light from the courtyard, his staff gathers daily for a simple seasonal lunch prepared by his two cooks, Asako Iwama and Lauren Maurer.

The Weather Project in Turbine Hall
of the Tate Modern, London, 2003.

PETER SELLARS (*director*): New Crowned Hope was a project of the City of Vienna to mark Mozart's 250th birthday. We invited visionary artists working in such politically intense locations as Congo, Cambodia, Paraguay, and Kurdistan to make new work based on the themes of Mozart's last year—magic and transformation, truth and reconciliation, and ceremonies for the dead. We commissioned six feature films, Mark Morris's Mozart Dances, John Adams's *A Flowering Tree,* and Alice Waters to create the Tables of New Crowned Hope.

Food is not a commodity but a culture, and farmers and chefs are artists. Food and architecture are the art forms that demand that you realize your highest ideals not on a canvas, not in a theater, not in a movie, but in the daily practice of your daily life.

Like Mozart, Alice Waters is fully committed to sophisticated and irresistible pleasure—delight with a powerful moral center. Fineness of detail, activated sensi-tivities and basic equality are the essential ingredients, leading to both a vision and a tangible reality of social justice, hard work, radical sharing, balanced lives, metabolisms, environmental footprints, and communities. Like Mozart, inside a world of sensationally awakened tastes and delirious fine feeling, Alice is feeding people radical ideas.

New Crowned Hope was a Masonic lodge in Vienna that counted Mozart and Haydn as members in which artists, intellectuals and activists discussed the possibilities of democracy over dinner. There was no democracy in Europe—there was only autocracy. Democracy had to first be imagined—it was politically dangerous—and to be made tangible and digestible by artists: Haydn and Mozart, for example, developed the string quartet, a powerful working model of equality. The new political reality always has to be prepared by artists—a generation later, everyone is dining off of it.

The Tables of New Crowned Hope were three long tables, each engaging one hundred people in pleasure, conversation, and surprise. Key figures in the power structure, including the future chancellor of Austria, dined freely with students, artists, and refugees. Intricate paper-cut banners from Francisco Toledo, created in communal workshops in radicalized Oaxaca, formed a lacy cloud canopy that declared its independence and interdependence overhead. Refugee musicians (memorably an astonishing Mongolian band) keep the air and our ears ringing with music.

A week later we had a weekend workshop on the future of the Edible Schoolyard in Europe with representatives from ten countries. The City of Rome stunned us all—they already requisition and supply organic food for the lunch of every school child in the city, empowering small organic farms and the next generation of young people in one amazing gesture.

the tables of
NEW CROWNED
HOPE, Vienna

NEW CROWNED HOPE

JENNIFER SHERMAN *(general manager, Chez Panisse)*: Whenever Alice calls I know it's going to be an adventure—an inspiring, tortuous, fabulous, once-in-a-lifetime adventure. She mentioned Vienna, lunch for one hundred and fifty at a school with an Edible Schoolyard, dinner for thirty in a two-hundred-year-old hunting lodge without electricity or running water and only fireplaces for cooking, and a final dinner for two hundred and fifty in the former stables of the royal palace, again with no kitchen. I said yes, of course.

I had to plan three different meals in three different venues with only my knives and Alice's assurances that "everything was taken care of." Somehow, through sheer will and Alice's charm, we attracted the most wonderful people to help us magically produce these beautiful and moving meals. Irene Weinfurter, Viennese artisanal caterer extraordinaire, was the linchpin of the events. She foraged burgundy-colored heirloom apples; fresh fat local ducks; a four-foot wheel of mountain cheese; trout from Alpine lakes, raised by a fisherman and his wife who came and proudly served their fish; green-black kale that we braised with new oil and garlic; a local pale-yellow bittersweet lettuce; *luftgetrockneter Schinken*, a local salty cured beef; garnet-colored beets; pumpkin oil; and the most fantastic imaginable variety of shell beans. A small and dedicated group of Chez Panisse chefs arrived over the next few days, bringing fresh energy and optimism.

I was worried about finding local food in the cold and dark of winter, so to prepare for the festival I joined Peter in Vienna the year before. We met with Barbara van Melle, a journalist committed to food justice and children's food education who is now the head of Slow Food in Austria. She helped us locate organic farmers and the Arche Noah, a regional center for biodiversity and a seed bank for thousands of heirloom varieties of vegetables, fruits, and grains, where we selected crops for the farmers to sow for the festival dinners the next year. One was a dinner out in the country at a place with no electricity—this was in the darkest time of the Viennese winter. Another was a big celebration in the city. I collaborated with Christina Kim on the design, which included tablecloths, hand-dyed prayer flags, and napkins. We wanted to create events that felt unique, where we could think about food in an unexpected context. I asked Peter if he would think about a little live music to introduce our last dinner. He didn't tell me in advance, but he arranged for wonderful Mongolian throat singers to perform.

"Knowledge is not value free...
the purpose of education is the
transmission of values."

Wes Jackson, the Land Institute

Yale Sustainable Food Project

In 2001, my daughter, Fanny, went to Yale. We walked into the dining commons and recognized that smell of reheated steam-table food. So when I met the president of Yale at freshman orientation I offered to help Yale's dining halls serve real food that was fresh, local, and organic. And I proposed that they start a school garden that would teach the same lessons at Yale that the Edible Schoolyard teaches in Berkeley.

JOSH VIERTEL *(president, Slow Food USA)*: I was farming on the East Coast when I met Alice. I told her about my commitment to the Slow Food movement, and she said, I'm trying to convince Yale University to transform its dining halls and start a farm, and I think you should go and help them. So I wrote the president of Yale a letter, proposing that they hire me to help create a sustainable food project. He agreed.

Six years later, I was hired to lead Slow Food USA and left the Yale Sustainable Food Project under the leadership of Melina Shannon-DiPietro, who was my codirector there. Together we had begun the transformation of the dining halls, creating seasonal menus and supporting local farmers. We had built academic programs so students could study food and farming in disciplines ranging from biology to political science. They could even major in food and agriculture as part of the Environmental Studies degree. And we had transformed the cultural life of the college, from start to finish. Freshman orientation now begins with trips to local organic farms, and at graduation, students garnish their graduation caps with bunches of radishes from the Yale farm.

My first spring in New Haven, students swung axes and machetes to clear brush and cut down trees. The farm we built, with terraces, fruit trees, and over three hundred varieties of vegetables, became the beating heart of the project. Students labored to build a wood-fired oven; they learned to bake real bread and pizza. The farm moved everyone. Students, senior faculty, captains of industry, grounds maintenance workers, dining service pot washers, and even Alice herself were transformed and refreshed by that place.

The weekend before I left, we built an open-air pavilion at the farm to provide a place for people to gather. In the tradition of a barn raising, students pulled together and raised the frame. Afterward, we feasted on a whole hog barbecue, and danced to bluegrass under the new roof. As I stepped back and watched the party, I knew I could leave and that it would continue without me. I could see future generations of young people at Yale learning what good food really is and where it comes from, learning to take joy in work, and learning not just to bake bread, but to share it.

"Be the change you want to see in the world."
Mohandas Gandhi

Once again, I was trying to open doors, break down walls, and stir things up. Here was an opportunity to feed people ideas on the Washington Mall, in the shadow of the Capitol.

JOAN NATHAN (*food writer, journalist*): We were planning the 2005 Food Culture USA event for the Smithsonian Folklife Festival, and my first idea was to ask Alice to build an Edible Schoolyard on the Mall. I wasn't sure how the Smithsonian would react to this, but they loved the idea. There are a few moments in life when your heart skips a beat, and watching an Edible Schoolyard being planted, with the Washington Monument to one side and the Capitol building on the other, was one of them for me. I had to call Alice and tell her. We were both so excited. I didn't realize what a big deal it would be to have Alice come to Washington. I didn't realize what a symbol she is until she got there and I saw the reaction the project got. It was a real step forward for this movement of food and education to lobby members of Congress at a lunch outdoors in the middle of the garden.

It was funny, too, because she has these impossibly high standards, and I was thinking, what a pain to have to get real cloth napkins and real plates and silverware, but it really made a difference. It made an impression. I think a lot of people on the East Coast are just beginning to think about food the way Alice does. This event helped. Many, many people visited while we were there. Even bureaucrats from the Department of Agriculture started coming by on their lunch hour. I thought, this is important, this is taking us one step further down the road to better food for everyone in America.

Senator Harkin of Iowa and Senator Clinton of New York lingered at the lunch table we had set up on the Mall. They were so knowledgeable about the issues. Both of them have taken strong stands: Senator Harkin in support of the Farm to School initiative, Senator Clinton in support of local agriculture in New York. I told them what I wanted—food that's good, clean, fair in every school—and they both understood where I was going—and that I didn't want to compromise.

MARK DANNER *(writer)*: The heat, the crickets, and the unlikely stalks of fresh corn planted on our nation's greensward: this is what I remember of that hot summer noontime on Washington Mall. This, and the half dozen political superstars gathered around that tiny picnic table in the bright sun. How do you manage to herd together the most powerful, sought-after legislators in the capital—including a soon-to-be majority leader and a future secretary of state—to direct their elusive attentions to the subjects of food, nutrition, and the health of the country's children? A simple question, which in the cosmos of Chez Panisse, The Edible Schoolyard, and Alice Waters has a simple answer: you lay out a lovely, simple table on the Mall and offer them some pizzetta. Very, very good pizzetta. And a bit of salad. Oh, and that dessert . . .

I remember clearly how each and every one of the political celebrities grouped around that wooden table that bright day in 2005 arrived with the apologetic reminder that he or she could remain only "a few minutes." The future secretary of state, the acknowledged political star among the half dozen and thus the last to arrive, left it to an aide to pronounce with practiced apologetic tone that the senator "could stay only twenty minutes, at most." The sun beat down. Hillary wore a hat, as did Nancy, and Alice. The table was tiny, and in the heat of the day I could hear the clicking of crickets interspersed among the distant car horns. Somewhere nearby in that most powerful of capitals powerful people were arguing and debating and denouncing and lobbying. Then the pizzetta arrived, and after a moment or two there was a bit of laughter and the conversation took off.

The talk began with a dramatic picture of a problem and then its solution simply and powerfully presented. The philosophy of The Edible Schoolyard and its magic: schoolchildren working in their own garden, shaping what they grew in the alchemy of their own kitchen. The need to spread that model across the country, not only as a clear and simple answer to childhood obesity and other food-related maladies but also to help revitalize education itself. To do that by working with the hands as well as the mind, to learn by doing. The answer was there, proven, functioning. And at the table, munching on their pizzetta, smiling through their salads, were the people who by virtue of their influence and their votes could spread it to every public school in the country.

Amid the drowsy heat, the intoxicating, delicate aromas, the discussion grew animated, took flight—we had long since left the appointed twenty minutes behind, were slipping past an hour as the peaches and figs arrived—and I happily realized that these lawmakers fully grasped the idea: they got it. Half the half dozen at the small table represented California, knew Chez Panisse and Alice well. And hard upon that happy realization came a sobering one: that knowing and understanding were only the beginning or not even; that the power of those at the table consisted as much in comprehending the power arrayed against them—the lobbies, the interests, the sheer inertia invested in the world as it is—and knowing not to threaten it, as it did in trying to change the world. Above the happy sated faces I could almost see the thought balloons floating and bobbing in the humid Washington air: "food lobby," "farm bill," "agriculture committee." Pick your battles—that was the thing. Exciting, even in the face of that revelation of what one already knew, to gaze on that irresistible force from California, smiling beneath the brim of her hat, batter eloquently, charmingly, and relentlessly against that immovable object from Washington. Impossible, watching that perfect little drama, not to realize that change, if it comes, when it comes, will owe its existence as much to a revolution in popular attitudes as it will to the beliefs of those elected and empowered to lead. Here leaders, however well fed, are followers. Disappointing perhaps, but to mourn the reality is like mourning the humidity in Washington. As I write, a new childhood nutrition bill—imperfect but an improvement—works its way through Congress, even as the first lady, with diligent schoolchildren as helpers, tends her White House garden. Revolutions spring from many sources, not least from a tiny wooden table, laden amid the crickets with delicious food, on a hot afternoon on the Washington Mall.

"Revolutions spring from many sources, not least from a tiny table laden with delicious food." Mark Danner

I'm sitting with Cathrine Sneed, who started the garden project at the San Francisco County jail; Senator Tom Harkin of Iowa, who started the Farm to School project; and Senator Hillary Clinton, who championed local, organic food in New York state.

turning up the heat

For the garden, we had to call all our East Coast friends, starting with Christopher Hirsheimer, who enlisted Jon Carloftis, the garden designer, who brought a truck full of trees; and Josh Viertel of the Yale Sustainable Food Project, who brought a team of people to help.

CHRISTINA KIM *(artist, owner of dosa)*: I had a feeling Alice's idea of making an edible garden on the Washington Mall would demonstrate her plan about food and education in a really dynamic way. I didn't know what I would do, but I wanted to be there to help. Going without any expectations, I thought of myself as support to the front line. I worked behind the scenes, making myself useful and making signs to hang on the vine-covered ramada where people were exchanging ideas. I remember being so impressed by the plants, growing in the heat, in the middle of that huge lawn. It was very hot! Everybody was so sweaty, but those little plants, the corn in the fields, looked so healthy and were just growing toward the sky. It was great to see so many interesting and enthusiastic young Americans gathering to help. And, then, at the end, we ate delicious pizza out of the wood oven! The experience helped me realize what is possible—what one person can do when there is a sense of unity.

edible

education

"In the long view, no nation is healthier than its children, or more prosperous than its farmers." Harry S. Truman

By now we understood two things about The Edible Schoolyard. First, the kids like the program very, very much. They know that this is happening because somebody cares about them. Second, we learned that when children participate in growing and cooking food, they all want to eat it.

ESTHER COOK *(chef teacher, The Edible Schoolyard)*: When I started at The Edible Schoolyard in 1997, with 850 kids who speak twenty-two different languages, I saw again what I'd seen teaching teenagers to cook after school in Oakland: that the most important part of this kind of project is not the cooking per se but how the cooking and feeding demonstrate to these kids that someone cares about them and respects them. The Edible Schoolyard has always been very successful not only at helping kids learn how to cook and grow things, but also at teaching them how to take care of, and feel better about, themselves. Every year I make valentines for every child in the school, and in that valentine I tell them, quite explicitly, that they are loved. To me, this is the most important thing a child can know; it is the basis for their self-esteem and their creativity.

When we first started The Edible Schoolyard, we remodeled the old cafeteria (*left*) and used it as our first kitchen classroom. Setting the table has always been an important ritual in each class. Once the table is set, kids feel welcomed and invited to sit down together. Many times they don't want to get up and go to their next class. One of my favorite pictures is of these three kids sitting together (*below left*), having a relaxed conversation. It doesn't even feel like they're at school. But they are, and you can tell they're enjoying it, and enjoying each other, for all the right reasons.

Esther Cook, chef teacher at The Edible Schoolyard (*right*), with two kitchen volunteers. Her teaching is beautiful to observe: she is deeply respectful of her students and cares deeply about them.

a delicious revolution

MARSHA GUERRERO (*director, The Edible Schoolyard*): Ten years ago I was living in Singapore and getting ready to return to the United States. While I was in Asia I had kept up with Alice's work, and I knew she had started a garden program at a public middle school in Berkeley. With my return looming, I wondered if there might be a place for me there, so I telephoned her. She encouraged me to come home and be part of the the support team that was shaping hands-on learning for more than eight hundred middle school students.

When I arrived in the fall of 2000, The Edible Schoolyard was already five years old and thriving under the leadership of David Hawkins and Esther Cook. I clearly remember my first visit to the garden with Alice. There were children engaged in a variety of interesting tasks, and an almost garish show of color—chards, lettuces, grains, flowers, bees, and butterflies. I was astonished by the

clusters of young people studying the land, on the land: hoisting tools, digging, sifting compost, and examining curling grubs. I recalled my middle school classroom science—dry-as-a-bone text-book learning. How fortunate these children are, I thought, to be in a limitless outdoor classroom, learning through their hands.

Alice and I walked to the kitchen classroom, where children were working on piles of rainbow chard and scallions. Fresh herbs and the fragrance of basmati rice filled the room. Esther came over to give us a quick explanation of the recipe, then briskly returned to her students to lend a hand or gently direct them as they carefully chopped and blanched and combined.

Over the many years since, I've watched a few thousand children taking their time in our one-acre garden. They learn where food comes from, growing and harvesting hundreds of pounds of

hundreds of varieties of vegetables, fruits, flowers, and herbs. In the kitchen classroom they work together to prepare, from the produce they have tended, something beautiful and delicious. Then they sit around the table together to eat, and talk and get to know one another a little better.

There is now an elegant history to this lush plot of urban land, a history deeply embedded in the culture of Martin Luther King, Jr., Middle School. A generation of kids has moved asphalt, made and spread compost, planted trees, built a toolshed, and laid the foundations for a green-house. They have cleared brush and moved 3,000-gallon tanks into place to catch the water that will irrigate the lower orchard. They have named and renamed chickens, carrying and caressing them. At King School today, food is an academic subject, children learn by doing, and beauty is a living language.

a universal idea

There are wonderful school gardens beginning to grow all across the country, and many cafeterias care about good food, but The Edible Schoolyard is about more than that—it's about tying all these things together and placing them at the center of a school's curriculum. There are several affiliated schools who understand this and have committed to this complete vision. Among them are: in New Orleans, the Samuel J. Green public charter school and the Arthur Ashe School; in Brooklyn, New York, P.S. 216, the Arturo Toscanini School; in Greensboro, North Carolina, the Greensboro Children's Museum; in Los Angeles, the Larchmont Charter Schools; and the Boys and Girls Clubs of San Francisco.

SAM LEVIN *(student, founder, Project Sprout)*: Every week we have Turnip Thursday. Every Thursday morning, before school, after harvesting for the cafeterias, my buddy Ben and I pull up a giant white turnip. We deliver the rest of the harvest, going our separate ways, and then meet up again in Latin class first period of the day, Ben usually holding the turnip and the knife. Ben sits down and starts slicing the turnip up. Ben's sort of a clown, and he'll usually say something like "Who wants a piece of this bad boy?" The rest of the kids in our class start laughing, and the hands go up. Ben starts throwing chunks of turnip across the room. Usually the teacher gets a piece, too. The first ten minutes of Latin every Thursday are filled with munching sounds. Some days, Ben has already cut a few pieces of the turnip off in the halls on his way to class, and usually there is leftover turnip after class, so the pieces get distributed to various corners of the school. The first day, about five weeks ago, that Ben and I brought a turnip with us, was because neither of us had eaten breakfast. But as we were slicing it up that first day, naturally someone in our class asked us what the hell we were doing with a giant white beet and a knife. Kids and teacher alike were skeptical the first day, but one kid mustered up the courage to try a piece. And it's been Turnip Thursday ever since. I've heard Thursday's turnip mentioned in history class, sociology class, and phys. ed. I've heard it talked about in the hallways, and seen pieces of turnip lying in mailboxes in the office. Last Thursday, Ben was late to class, and before he got there, someone asked me if I brought a backup turnip. Some Wednesdays, I get special requests to reserve a piece of turnip for the following day. I'm considering putting together a waiting list.

This brings up a question I have been trying to answer for the past two years. How do you get from Turnip Thursdays to excitement over fresh food every day? How do you get from one garden, in one school, to a country that eats and lives in a very different way? It's not an easy question to answer, but I think if there were ever a time when we were ready to answer that question, it would be now. So let's try.

ALICE WATERS

Edible Schoolyard
A UNIVERSAL IDEA

When Sam Levin was only thirteen, he started a school garden at his public school in Massachusetts that invigorates the entire curriculum and now helps supply the cafeteria. It's completely run by students. Three more Project Sprouts have already started and more are on the way.

awareness

diversity

taste

patience

wonder

inspiration

pride

orderliness

imagination

respect

gratitude

empathy

values in place

interdependence

preparedness

enthusiasm

beauty

The Principles of Edible Education

Food Is an Academic Subject

A school garden, kitchen, and cafeteria are a key part of the core curriculum, teaching that ecology and gastronomy are integral to every subject, from reading and writing to science and art.

School Lunch Is for Every Child

Good food is a right, not a privilege, and all children deserve a universal free school lunch. In the middle of each school day, they eat a delicious, healthy meal, appreciating another way of eating.

Schools Support Communities

School cafeterias buy fresh seasonal food from local, sustainable farms and ranches to stimulate and strengthen local food economies.

Children Learn by Doing

Hands-on education empowers children to learn more about the world they live in and share their newfound knowledge and appreciation of food.

Beauty Is a Language About Caring

A beautifully prepared environment, where deliberate thought goes into everything from garden paths to setting the table, communicates to children the deeply valuable message that we care about them, and in turn, it inspires them to care for others.

Cailey Cole

hope after Katrina

The photo shows me and Tony Recasner, the principal of Samuel J. Green School in New Orleans. Tony started The Edible Schoolyard program there in the wake of Hurricane Katrina. For the restaurant's thirty-fifth birthday we had a New Orleans-style benefit to raise funds for the new Edible Schoolyard, complete with an all-day sidewalk "Café du Monde" serving beignets and café au lait.

DAVIA NELSON (NPR's Kitchen Sisters): During The Edible Schoolyard Washington lobbying lunches, several of the senators and representatives suggested that Alice start another Edible Schoolyard, this one in the South, where juvenile obesity and diabetes were off the charts and where it would be closer to Washington so more elected officials might visit. Alice and I talked about it. We thought, where in the South was the confluence of a school, a principal, and a supportive community?

Later, on New Year's Day, we were sitting in Alice's kitchen. It was just five months after Katrina, and I was headed to New Orleans with my tape recorder. "New Orleans. That's where the next Edible Schoolyard belongs," Alice said. "They're starting from scratch, we could help in the rebuilding. Find me an angel there who can make this happen." Two hours after I'd landed I found myself gathered around a dinner table with Randy Fertel—a writer, activist, philanthropist, and a great cook who'd grown up in New Orleans. We started talking about Katrina and the aftermath, and I told him Alice's idea, and in a split second he said, "I know just the school. I know just the principal. I'm in." We picked up the phone and called Alice. The New Orleans Edible Schoolyard began.

239

It was important for me to write a book that was basic and principled and accessible. All of the Chez Panisse cookbooks so far were about the food at the restaurant. There's nothing wrong with that, but many of the recipes were for the kind of food people would only cook on special occasions. I thought it was time to put together a teaching cookbook that was about the food we actually eat at home, complete with lessons for the routine preparations that every home cook should be able to execute without having to look up the recipe.

ALICE WATERS

THE ART OF SIMPLE FOOD

Notes, Lessons, and Recipes from a Delicious Revolution

SAMANTHA GREENWOOD *(Chez Panisse special events chef)*: The idea behind *The Art of Simple Food* was always to step outside the restaurant framework and teach people how to cook at home.

I actually use the cookbook a lot. As that famous quotation from Robert Louis Stevenson says, "Every book is, in an intimate sense, a circular letter to the friends of him who writes it." Well, that's the way I feel about cookbooks. If I need to hear Kelsie Kerr I look in *The Art of Simple Food* (she wrote the lessons for Alice). If I need to hear David Tanis, I look in his books: the Café cookbook, *A Platter of Figs and Other Recipes,* and *Heart of the Artichoke.* I think of these kinds of books as love letters from intimate friends and coworkers.

The Art of Simple Food was written as a kind of instructional manual for our kids and other people who were just starting to cook. When Patty Curtan was writing it, her son Zach would call her from the army base where he was stationed and ask, "How do I roast a chicken?" and she would explain, and that would go in the book. Knowing that the people who work at Chez Panisse, who live on modest incomes, can cook this way at home and feed their families is proof to me that the idea of cooking this way really is possible.

forward to basics

the Rome Sustainable

Food Project

AT THE AMERICAN ACADEMY

I never imagined I would have an opportunity to revitalize the food program at an institution like the American Academy in Rome, which is beautifully sited amid gardens where Galileo demonstrated his telescope in 1611, on the summit of the Janiculum, the second-highest hill in Rome. The Academy is rooted in the values of scholarship—a perfect place to serve forth the thesis of edible education. Integrating a sustainable food project into the Academy's mission would feed fresh local food to artists and scholars working at the highest level, encouraging conviviality and enriching the free exchange of ideas across disciplines.

Left: In the Academy's gardens with Giovanni Bernabei, a farmer who supplies much of the Academy's produce, Mona Talbott, and Adele Chatfield-Taylor. Below left: A picture taken at a special dinner at the Academy in May 2010 that brought together (*from left to right, with hoes*) the American ambassador to Italy, David H. Thorne; the founder of Slow Food, Carlo Petrini; and the mayor of Rome, Giovanni Alemanno. In the middle of dinner, inspiration struck and everyone agreed to collaborate on a garden project on the Piazza di Campidoglio, right outside the mayor's office. The hoes they are holding were specially made and given to them by Giovanni Bernabei.

MONA TALBOTT (*director, Rome Sustainable Food Project*): The American Academy, founded in 1894, is a center for academic research and a home to American scholars and artists who have won the Rome Prize. During the last twenty years, under the guidance of Adele Chatfield-Taylor, president and CEO, the Academy has restored ten historic buildings and eleven acres of gardens, endowed the Rome Prize fellowships, professionalized the staff on both sides of the Atlantic, and generally rebuilt the institution. The Academy's tradition was that Fellows worked independently all day and over lunch and dinner engaged in passionate discussions at the table, sharing ideas and scholarship. But in recent years, everyone had stopped coming to meals. It was a paradox: why, in a country known for its gastron-

omy, was an institution like the Academy serving bland institutional food?

In May 2006, Alice asked me to head the Rome Sustainable Food Project. The immediate work was to bring the Roman countryside into the Academy, reconnect agriculture and culture, and inspire a return to the table. Frankly, I was nervous; I didn't speak a word of Italian. But I loved cooking the Mediterranean's nutritious cuisine of greens, grains, and beans; and after leaving Chez Panisse in 1997, I had worked mainly as a private chef and caterer for artists and scholars. The opportunity—to live in Rome and develop a working model for institutional dining—was irresistible.

When I arrived in August, Carmela Franklin, the director, led me into the Bass Garden, a walled

Views of the buildings and grounds of the American Academy.

245

paradise where we picked and ate ripe figs. La dolce vita! For six months I sourced ingredients, convinced stubborn local organic farmers to deliver, studied traditional Roman cuisine, and learned Italian. Two months before we took over, Alice sent Chris Boswell, a cook from Chez Panisse. Chris speaks Italian, is passionate about Italy, and is an excellent cook. We started an internship program, which adds youthful enthusiasm and vitality to the community and is a viable solution to complicated Italian labor issues.

On February 26, 2007, the project cooked its first meal for the residents. We grilled bread in the dining room fireplace and served an antipasto of *ricotta di pecora* and olives. We cooked chicken *alla mattone, farro* and *cavolo nero,* and a citrus compote and an olive oil cake made with the Academy's own olive oil. Our immediate goal was to bring people back to the table. Our bigger mission was to build an economically viable dining program to stimulate both work and conviviality.

TEDDY SZEMBERG O'CONNOR *(engineering student):* I just finished a month-long cooking internship at the Academy. I thought I'd be a cog in the kitchen machine, chopping to order. Instead, Mona and Chris made me stop and think, and use all my senses. I learned to feel for the perfect ripeness of tomatoes and to hear the purr of the beetroot telling me how to release its flavor.

Our daily meetings in the kitchen were a history lesson in Italian cooking. One day pasta expert Oretta Zanini de Vita showed us something extraordinary. She gingerly took out a piece of finest gauze—the rare handmade pasta called *filindeu* (veil of God), so delicately woven it made us almost stop breathing for fear of breaking it. Another day, while we were chopping greens, the most beautiful sound wafted in. We followed the music and found John Kamitsuka, the classical pianist, giving an informal recital. Sadly, after a while we had to get back to work or lunch wouldn't be on the table. These lessons from the Academy will stay with me for life.

247

ADELE CHATFIELD-TAYLOR *(president and CEO, American Academy in Rome)*: For the last twenty years, we have tried various experiments to improve the food at the American Academy in Rome. It was an urgent need for many reasons, particularly because the community gathers at mealtime daily, and the cross-fertilization among the fellows, for which the institution is known, cannot occur unless they are made happy and nurtured by being there. All experiments failed until we asked Alice Waters to get involved. She replied that she would do it if we would support a complete culinary revolution, because she was not interested in simply upgrading the menu. We enthusiastically agreed, knowing that this was the only way to go, and that Alice was the only person who could devise the plan. She recruited Mona Talbott, without whom the next two years would have been unimaginable. Mona is our talented, tireless, and inspired executive chef. She found and put all the pieces in place—with advice from Alice along the way—and since February 2007, our life has been transformed by the Rome Sustainable Food Project. The numbers of people campaigning to be present for lunch, Monday through Saturday, have tripled. Invitations are now met with glee. Our workdays have been energized, our conversation enriched, and our health improved. Mealtime is no longer a mundane ordeal but a joyous and delicious occasion among friends.

theater in a butcher shop

To visit Dario Cecchini's shop is more like going to a little theater than to a butcher. Dario is constantly trying to engage people in the preservation of their culture. His love for Dante is on a continuum with his love for traditional Tuscan *salumi*. He believes that we need it all: both divine poetry and delicious *sopressata*. But he allows for some innovation, too: he wanted to offer an affordable lunch for all the workers in Panzano, so he started selling grilled ground beef patties that he calls McDario burgers.

JOHN MEIS *(Tuscany consultant)*: About fifteen years ago during one of Alice's many visits to my part of Tuscany, I brought her to Dario Cecchini's butcher shop not far from where I live. I knew they had to meet. It was written. I introduced her simply as a friend from Berkeley. After about two minutes I could sense Alice was seduced—by the opera playing in the background, the aromas of rosemary and fennel and sage, the sensual array of fresh and cured meats and, of course, by Dario himself. We were going out to dinner that evening and she was leaving the next morning, so we did not intend to buy anything. But at one point she said, "Oh, I just love his little papers [to wrap up meat]. Do you think he would give me some?" Then, a few minutes later, "Oh, I love those divine little towels [old-fashioned hemp kitchen towels]. Do you think I could buy one?" Dario did not say much during that visit, but it was obvious something of consequence had sparked between the two of them.

She returned to Dario's shop a year later, this time during a longer stay in the area, and came back not with papers or towels, but with an entire Sardinian sheep. On this occasion Dario was reciting Dante while his "customers" drank wine and feasted on larded crostini. And Alice had an "epiphany"—her word. Unaware of the event, that evening at supper I ventured to say, "But sometimes you just want to go in and buy your meat and be on your way." Bad mistake. "John," she admonished me, "you just don't get it. Dario is more than a butcher." And indeed he is.

Since then we have been back to Dario's many times, and each time the atmosphere becomes charged with a kind of vital energy. Apart from a little French, their relationship is practically nonverbal, but when together they exude deep mutual respect and esteem, a palpable love of food and fun, and lots of eye twinkle. Lots. Alice and Dario are soul mates. I got it.

CORBY KUMMER (*journalist, writer*): In 2004, Carlo Petrini, the founder and head of Slow Food, came up with another of his crazy ideas: bring together four thousand farmers and food producers from all over the world, many of whom had never left their own village let alone country, and introduce them to one another, to learn how much they have in common and how much they could teach one another.

Like much of what Petrini had come up with in the past, it was a noble, impossible scheme, and he wouldn't let it go until his associates got it done. This meant having local chapters raise the money for transport of people from 131 countries, and mobilizing the entire city of Turin, the regional capital near Slow Food's birthplace, to open its doors to visitors from around the world: Petrini insisted that the farmers stay in people's homes, not hotels.

Terra Madre was a huge success both despite and because of the logistical obstacles: on the long bus rides to and from the towns and villages where they were staying, some in the mountains of Piedmont, agave and vanilla farmers from Mexico would meet one another—and meet sesame producers from Burkina Faso. Olive growers in Israel and Palestine would come together in a place where they could talk and exchange ideas, and plan future collaborations (this happened). It didn't matter whether or not they shared a common language. They made themselves understood. And the spectacle and pageantry of the planetary gatherings—a term that acquired real significance in the case of Terra Madre— underscored what Petrini wanted from the start: a sense of dignity and importance for people who had never felt themselves important on the world stage. Speakers who came to address them— Prince Charles, Vandana Shiva, Petrini of course, and Alice Waters—all conveyed the sense that the truly important people that kept the world alive were the people in the audience. Petrini was especially satisfied that the FAO [Food and Agriculture Organization of the United Nations] and the European Union were represented, demonstrating that the world's official governing boards were listening, too.

For anyone who roams the halls of Terra Madre, the sheer profusion of faces is as moving as any of the stirring addresses—including a charismatic fifteen-year-old farm leader named Sam Levin, who opened the 2008 edition. The power of the gathering is inspiring other counries to organize their own Terra Madres: Ireland, Brazil, and the Netherlands so far, and Petrini now won't let go till ten thousand farmers gather near the Statue of Liberty. If anyone can make the impossible happen, it's Carlo— and, as you'll see on the following pages, his frequent co-conspirator, Alice.

Terra Madre was an earthshaking experience for me. One hundred and thirty-one countries, five thousand people. It was like the Tower of Babel in a way, because with so many languages, how could there be enough translators? But we understood one another just the same. It was a summit conference for our Mother Earth's most responsible stewards, whose priorities transcend boundaries of all kinds.

Carlo Petrini is one of the greatest communicators of our age, and one of its great humanitarians and egalitarians.

CARLO PETRINI (*founder, Slow Food International*): Alice shares with me the passion for a slow revolution that is involving the world. And together we want to involve it more. In 1988, on my first trip to California, I wanted to meet Alice and eat at Chez Panisse—at any cost. At the time, it wasn't the least bit easy to find a restaurant that married sustainable, carefully researched ingredients with the supreme quality of its cooking.

We immediately found we were in sync and started a friendship and collaboration that has only grown and gotten deeper, in ideas, projects, and exchanges. I wanted her immediately to commit herself to Slow Food, and I must say that the commitment she unhesitatingly showed had been fundamental to Slow Food's widespread diffusion across the United States.

No one has Alice's energy, her fertile inventiveness, and limitless passion for food, farming, and nature's marvelous products. It was Alice who introduced me to American farmers' markets and the movement of amazing people fighting for good, clean, and fair food in their houses, their cafeterias, their children's schools, and for future generations. In 2000 Alice took me to visit The Edible Schoolyard at the Martin Luther King, Jr., Middle School in Berkeley and I was thunderstruck: here was a perfect model for Slow Food to spread all over the world. It's thanks to her

example that, through Slow Food, school gardens are now growing everywhere, at every latitude.

She's helped me from the beginning with Terra Madre, the worldwide network of food communities that met for the first time in 2004 in Turin and since then has become a strong, active network in 153 countries with thousands of food communities—communities of people who put food at the center of their lives as an element of revolution. Wherever I go I find farmers and cooks, young and old, who with only their work, pride, and determination are building something epochal from their fields and their kitchens.

The start of anything is always an adventure, and always with the feeling of "Can we really do it?" So many times Alice and I have found ourselves at the start of an adventure—and I think for her it's been that way since the moment she gave life to Chez Panisse. We've both become a bit less uncertain, a bit more grown-up. But what has never changed for either of us is a strong belief in what you do and what you project for the future—in the possibility of a better food system that will bring greater happiness in the service of everyone. Today Slow Food is a strong, thriving international network. I'm happy to have shared so much of the path to getting there with Alice—and I'm sure that in the future the slow revolution will go much, much farther.

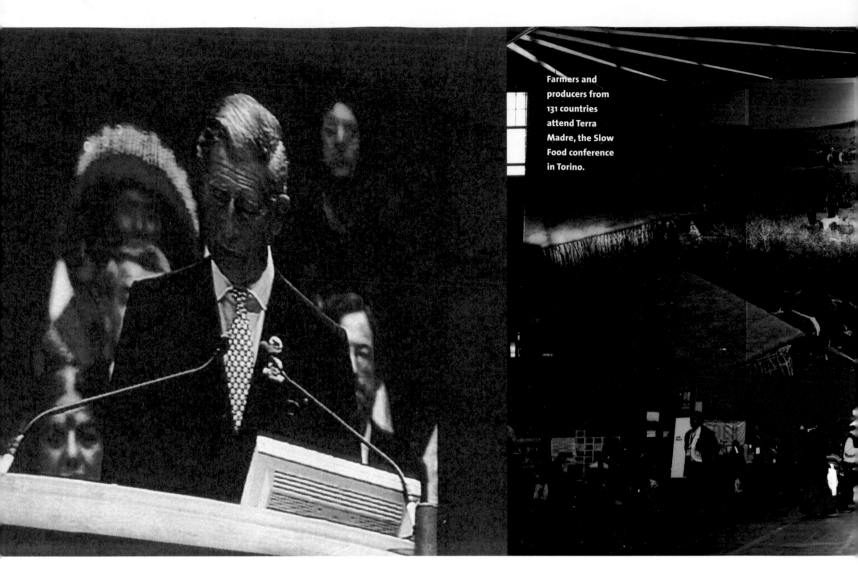

Farmers and producers from 131 countries attend Terra Madre, the Slow Food conference in Torino.

"UNIFORMITY IS NOT NATURE'S WAY.

DIVERSITY IS NATURE'S WAY." Vandana Shiva

SLOW FOOD NATION

ERIC SCHLOSSER *(writer)*: Slow Food Nation was a gathering of the tribes, an event that attracted organic farmers, food safety activists, home gardeners, school gardeners, locavores, vegans, ranchers committed to humane animal husbandry, and a great many people who like good food. More than 80,000 of them showed up in San Francisco during September of 2008, proving that what had begun as a counterculture was entering the mainstream.

One of the most encouraging parts of the event, for me, was the inclusion of farm workers and their representatives—and the strong declaration that this movement wasn't created to benefit an elite but to build a new, fair food system.

In retrospect, was Slow Food Nation just another Bay Area foodie celebration? Did its impact end once the speeches were over and the taste pavilions torn down? I don't think so. Less than a year after its organizers planted an edible, organic victory garden in front of San Francisco's Civic Center, organic gardens bloomed at the White House and at the headquarters of the United States Department of Agriculture. The revolution that Alice Waters helped to set in motion had finally spread from Berkeley to the Beltway. Beyond the symbolism, a great deal still needs to be done. But a cultural shift has occurred, much like the rise of the environmental movement forty years ago, and the momentum now seems unstoppable.

We organized Slow Food Nation because I thought it was time to have an all-American event that emulated both Terra Madre and the Slow Food conclave called Il Salone del Gusto, where people get to taste all kinds of artisanal foods worth saving. One of the Slow Food Nation events was this panel, probably the most inimidating and wonderful panel I've ever been on. From left to right: Michael Pollan, Vandana Shiva, Eric Schlosser, Wendell Berry, Corby Kummer (the moderator), me, Carlo Petrini, and Carlo's translator.

eat-in

SLOW FOOD NATION, LABOR DAY, 2008, DOLORES PARK

DAVID PRIOR *(Chez Panisse Foundation communications director, writer)*: I was studying at Slow Food's University of Gastronomic Science in Bra, Italy, when I met the organizers of Slow Food Nation. Staging such an event in the home of fast food was something I knew I had to be part of. I applied for an internship and was thrown into the deep end—in the United States for the first time, an Australian with little or no knowledge of the Bay Area. My role was to organize the Come to the Table Dinner for six hundred in front of City Hall that opened the event. But it was the closing event, a little side project, the Eat-In at Dolores Park, that will stay with me forever.

I developed the Eat-In with my friend Gordon Jenkins, an alumnus of the Yale Sustainable Food Project. Gordon and I couldn't be more different, but we share the same commitment to food justice and the same concern for the future of food. We knew that Slow Food Nation was drawing hundreds of young farmers, chefs, students, and activists. Optimistic, energetic, and more than a little naïve, we set out to make as big a statement as possible with a dramatic gathering on Labor Day, the final day of Slow Food Nation. Alice said, "My dear, we can't think narrowly. We have to think in the biggest possible way." So we did.

We decided to stage an eat-in in Dolores Park. We erected a long table for three hundred, built a stage with a platform of hay bales and a barn-shaped proscenium arch painted red, and asked people to open up their kitchens and invite perfect strangers to come and cook with them, using leftover produce from the farmers' market. People cooked beans harvested from the victory garden in front of city hall and bicycled to the park balancing their offerings on their handlebars. We asked activists and farmers to deliver their messages (among them fifteen-year-old farmer-activist Sam Levin, making his first major public appearance), and every person signed the tablecloth with a simple pledge. At the time I knew nothing about the Free Speech Movement and the political and cultural resonance of calling something an "eat-in" in the Bay Area. I just wanted to be part of a social change in the making. I think I was.

261

farming = liberty

VICTORY GARDEN, CIVIC CENTER PLAZA, SAN FRANCISCO

planted the seeds of change

KATRINA HERON (*journalist*): A victory garden grew in front of City Hall in the 1940s, which added a certain historical logic to Slow Food Nation's petition that we roll up the manicured lawn on Civic Center Plaza and throw an extended green party. Sown in July 2008 by friends and volunteers, the circular planting beds of this victory garden covered one-third of an acre with organic vegetables, fruits, herbs, and flowers that by Labor Day made for a kind of horticultural fireworks display. It was the obvious centerpiece for a national celebration of food and sustainable agriculture, yet the garden seemed at first surprisingly out of place—incongruous, even, ringed as it was by the massive stone and glass edifices of an urban grid and surrounded by politely clipped municipal hedges. We're no longer used to seeing our food growing before our eyes, much less in a public setting. Runner beans, sunflowers, and corn tassels zoomed skyward against the backdrop of the Rotunda, while carrots and beets and lettuces and tomatoes literally ran circles around one another along the furrows. Masses of bright flowers came close to rioting. The whole scene hummed with insect and bird life, color and ripeness (harvests were donated to the San Francisco Food Bank).

It was a secret garden, hidden in plain sight. People came upon it unawares and were astonished, stopped dead in their tracks, wanting to know how on earth it could have gotten here. Whether they were out for a jaunt or on their way to get married, the garden interrupted them into reverie. Once inside the gate, they stood still and smiled, and turned in slow circles. Then began conversations of all kinds and in many languages about seeds and cultivars, the ways of soil and pollinators, other gardens that were or had been beloved.

As is the way of such things, just about the time the garden seemed to have settled into the neighborhood and was offering those subliminal reassurances of being there when you came back, it was gone. Slow Food Nation wound down, the stage was struck, and a long rectangle of turf was rolled out again, like a coat of dull paint. Not that long ago, I heard someone who was walking across the plaza say, "There used to be a beautiful garden here. I wonder what happened to it?"

ANYA FERNALD (*food activist and executive director, Slow Food Nation*): At the heart of the hustle and pulse of Slow Food Nation, I felt very calm and thrilled about the future. All the urgency for radical change had created this vast, wonderful moment where I could feel that better food might be in the future for America.

As the director of Slow Food Nation, my head and life had been filled with a thousand daily decisions and fluctuations, but during the days of the event itself I was able to lean back and become part of the experience we had all created. What I felt about that experience was that if—for just a moment—a whole city was talking about food, about being creative and daring in thinking about how they were going to change food, then there was the possibility that soon our whole country could be changing the way we eat.

I remember people telling me excitedly about a connection they had made in sourcing pickles for a taste pavilion, about the urban gardening group they'd met at the Changemaker's Day event, the person they had not seen in years who they bumped into over the beans in the victory garden—it was as if all our kind had come out of their various forests, and only then did we realize how many we numbered, how big our power could be. What had felt peripheral to me before that event seemed to move to center stage, and we could be very, very hopeful.

The opening-night dinner of Slow Food Nation took place in front of City Hall. It was cooked by scores of volunteers. The banqueters waited on themselves. It was the most intimate dinner for six hundred I have ever shared. In the shots above (*center row, top to bottom*): Anya Fernald eating oysters; John Bela, designer of the garden in front of City Hall; me with Sarah Weiner, who was a project director, and Sylvan Brackett, who oversaw Slow Food on the Go.

creating green kitchens

Clockwise from top left: me with the mayor of San Francisco, Gavin Newsom; Dieter Kosslick and Tommy Struck of the Berlin International Film Festival; Carlo Petrini and blacksmith-forager Angelo Garro; the members of the production team of our Green Kitchen demonstrations; me and ecological activist and philosopher Vandana Shiva.

Almost ten years ago my wife and I visited Alice, who was staying in a village in the mountains of Corsica with some friends of hers, among them David Tanis, one of the contributors to *In the Green Kitchen*. There was not much to do there, but there was an ancient wood-burning bread oven near the house, and David taught me how to make bread by hand. I had never thought of myself as a cook before, much less a baker, but when I got home I couldn't stop myself—I started taking classes and reading books and baking every day. I even built a bread oven in my backyard. The whole culture of our family changed because of what I was doing.

I've been a member of the board of the Chez Panisse Foundation for over ten years, and giving this kind of experience to children is what we're working to support—an experience that is not only practical, beneficial, and fun, but also one that wakes them up to themselves and their world and helps them feel engaged, purposeful, and aware of their surroundings and what they can give. Not only do the kids change, but their schools change, too.

I was recently made president of the San Francisco Recreation and Park Commission. I've begun to wonder how what we do at The Edible Schoolyard could be applied to San Francisco's parks, and not only there, but to state parks and even to our national parks. The values of sustainability, preservation, and care are already enshrined in our parks, and it just seems natural to me that these values should be extended to food programs and concessions for the education and pleasure of children and their families.

At Slow Food Nation, we built a simple kitchen, minimally equipped, where short demonstrations of simple recipes and basic techniques were given by nearly thirty cooks, including Darina Allen, who came all the way from Ireland. We asked each participant to keep it uncomplicated, and we made short videos of some of the presentations. I persuaded my friends Christopher Hirsheimer and Melissa Hamilton to photograph the cooks for the book that grew out of the collaboration, *In the Green Kitchen*.

world premiere of *Food, Inc.*
BERLIN FILM FESTIVAL

berlin film festival jury

BUILDING CONSENSUS

They made me a juror at the 2009 Berlin Film Festival! It was a dream come true, in a way, but so unlikely and humbling to be impaneled with the extraordinary people who were fellow jurors. The jury is pictured opposite; from left, Spanish film director Isabel Coixet; Gaston Kaboré, the filmmaker from Burkina Faso; British actress Tilda Swinton; American director Wayne Wang; myself; the late German film, theater, and opera director Christoph Schlingensief; and Swedish crime novelist and playwright Henning Mankell. I was changed by our deliberations, which were intense and deeply serious. It was a struggle and a joy to be part of this process, and it taught me something about collaborations: if you begin with a shared set of values, and you care enough about making something happen, you can reach a consensus even if you're bitterly divided when you start. The picture on the right is of Michael Pollan, who had traveled to Berlin for the premiere of *Food, Inc.*

DIETER KOSSLICK (*director, Berlin International Film Festival*): Alice has always lived close to the movies. From the restaurant's earliest days, Alice cooked for filmmakers, both local heroes like Francis Ford Coppola and George Lucas, and Old World migrants like Jean-Luc Godard, Wim Wenders, and Werner Herzog.

In 2006, the Berlinale called Alice, together with her Slow Food friends Vandana Shiva and Carlo Petrini, to join a program on Hunger, Food, and Taste, the beginning of a cultural recipe exchange among the three big Bs of food, Berkeley, Berlin, and Bra, the hometown of Carlo Petrini and Slow Food. In 2008, a new section of the film festival was begun, called Culinary Cinema, under the direction of Tommy Struck. A highlight of this exchange was discovering the powerful documentary, *Food, Inc.*, by Robert Kenner, Michael Pollan, and Eric Schlosser, which I first saw in the picturesque forge of Angelo Garro, a blacksmith and a forager for Chez Panisse. The film was shown at the Berlinale 2009 to an audience of eighteen hundred and later earned an Oscar nomination. The same year Alice was on the festival's International Jury. Alice's temperament evokes associations of silk and steel, of a shimmering tablecloth and gleaming cutlery. And what's on the table? We think it's a tree-ripened, good, clean, fair, and beautiful peach.

luminous curtain
AT THE BRANDENBURG GATE

CLARE PTAK *(owner, Violet Cakes)*: Working with David Tanis and David Lindsay was like being on laughing gas. David L. had sourced beautiful organic apples for the tarts and greens for the lasagne; for the sauce, David T. brought black truffles from France, packed in rice in his suitcase. We tasted twenty-five loaves to find the right bread for the grilled cheese sandwiches. I drank buttermilk out of the carton in the back of the van, driving through snow-covered Berlin looking for the next market. Some of us had never worked together before, but it didn't matter. Making buttermilk ice cream and apple tarts with Patty Curtan and her daughter Rose was a dream. So was sharing minicupcakes with Tilda Swinton's angelic children. We kept the magnums of Bandol rosé cold out on the porch overlooking the curtain.

DIETER KOSSLICK *(director, Berlin International Film Festival)*: Eight o'clock P.M., February 12, 2010: the snow had stopped falling, covering the square with an immaculate white carpet. Around one thousand people had gathered in front of the Brandenburg Gate, which was hidden by a colorful curtain made of recycled billboards, turning the square into an open-air movie theater. Twenty-one years ago, here people were literally tearing down the Berlin Wall. Now they watched a giant patchwork rising to unveil a masterpiece of cinema, *Metropolis*, by Fritz Lang, shown after more than eighty years for the first time in a complete version. In a room overlooking the gate and the screen Alice was serving dinner to Christina Kim and the seamstresses who had created the curtain. Alice's team prepared soup from turnips and beets, vegetable lasagne, and buttermilk ice cream. It's hard to uphold Alice's fresh and local food standards in Berlin in February. But don't expect compromises from her when it comes to food.

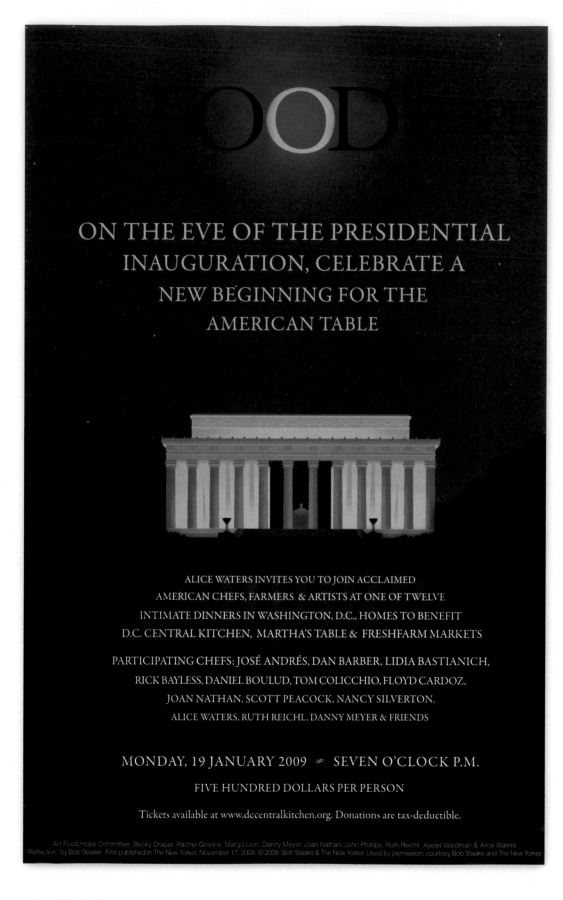

ON THE EVE OF THE PRESIDENTIAL
INAUGURATION, CELEBRATE A
NEW BEGINNING FOR THE
AMERICAN TABLE

ALICE WATERS INVITES YOU TO JOIN ACCLAIMED
AMERICAN CHEFS, FARMERS & ARTISTS AT ONE OF TWELVE
INTIMATE DINNERS IN WASHINGTON, D.C., HOMES TO BENEFIT
D.C. CENTRAL KITCHEN, MARTHA'S TABLE & FRESHFARM MARKETS

PARTICIPATING CHEFS: JOSÉ ANDRÉS, DAN BARBER, LIDIA BASTIANICH,
RICK BAYLESS, DANIEL BOULUD, TOM COLICCHIO, FLOYD CARDOZ,
JOAN NATHAN, SCOTT PEACOCK, NANCY SILVERTON,
ALICE WATERS, RUTH REICHL, DANNY MEYER & FRIENDS

MONDAY, 19 JANUARY 2009 ✍ SEVEN O'CLOCK P.M.

FIVE HUNDRED DOLLARS PER PERSON

Tickets available at www.dccentralkitchen.org. Donations are tax-deductible.

Art.Food.Hope Committee: Becky Draper, Rachel Goslins, Margo Lion, Danny Meyer, Joan Nathan, John Phillips, Ruth Reichl, Ayelet Waldman & Alice Waters
"Reflection" by Bob Staake. First published in The New Yorker, November 17, 2008. © 2008 Bob Staake & The New Yorker. Used by permission, courtesy Bob Staake and The New Yorker.

The president-elect called for a national day of service on Martin Luther King, Jr.'s birthday. I decided to go back to Washington, D.C., and collaborate on a benefit for D.C. Central Kitchen, Martha's Table, and Freshfarm Markets—three community organizations that feed and empower the hungry. We staged dinners that brought artists, writers, and food people to the table with supporters of the new administration. The people who opened up their homes for us to use for the benefit dinners were unbelievably hospitable; all the chefs who participated were welcomed in extraordinary ways. Best of all, the settings enabled the kind of intimate conversation that is impossible at typical gala benefits.

Bob Staake kindly allowed us to alter his shimmering *New Yorker* cover for this invitation.

benefit at the Phillips Collection

SARAH WEINER (*founder, Seedling Projects*): The inauguration was in six weeks. Six weeks to recruit chefs, find waiters, sell hundreds of tickets, source local produce in the dead of an East Coast winter, and book flights for the Chez Panisse SWAT team. And find accommodations for every visiting chef and their out-of-town kitchen staff. The day before the presidential inauguration. With no budget.

Once the chefs were in, we were ready to go. With a team led by food writer Joan Nathan and novelist Ayelet Waldman, we went to work. Henriot was soon in for over $10,000 worth of Champagne, and Whole Foods was good-naturedly bullied into donating all the pantry items we couldn't source from local farms. We began to gather volunteer waiters and prep cooks and the last available Champagne flutes in the greater D.C. area.

Over two hundred tickets were spoken for before sales went live. We planned to cap the number of sales at near the actual number of seats, but we didn't know how many seats there would be, because I was still trying to coax some of our hosts into squeezing another five or ten into their homes. And, of course, we needed to save some seats for last-minute friends and luminaries.

We estimated, we planned, and we sold. A little voice in my head kept saying, "Danger!" but I paid no heed. A week later it happened, "We're up to 520! What do I do? Can't Bob Woodward take ten more? Can't everyone take ten more?" We solved that crisis: "Book the Phillips Collection!" On January 19, 2009, twelve of the most wonderful chefs in the country descended on twelve of the most dignified homes in Washington, D.C.—and the Phillips Collection—in what the *New York Times* called "the hottest ticket at the inauguration." And we raised over $100,000 for D.C. food banks and farmers' markets.

ART FOOD HOPE

bay leaves for an inauguration

The Edible Schoolyard sent a care package with a wreath of bay leaves to wish us good luck. Christina Kim came to lend a hand and wove a bay leaf onto each place card. David Lindsay came from Switzerland. Claire Ptak and my daughter, Fanny, flew in from London. Doug Hamilton (*far left*) was also part of this extraordinary team of people.

DOUG HAMILTON (*film producer and director*): In 2003, I directed a film biography of Alice for American Masters, the Public Television series that celebrates the lives and the creative processes of America's outstanding cultural artists. While the show was a much-deserved celebration of Alice's life and the accomplishments of Chez Panisse, there was something far more significant about it. It was a recognition—by one of America's great cultural institutions—of the connection between food and culture. It seems that we had finally arrived at a time when the link between the artistry that goes into every plate at Chez Panisse was acknowledged nationally as much more than just the way to a delicious meal.

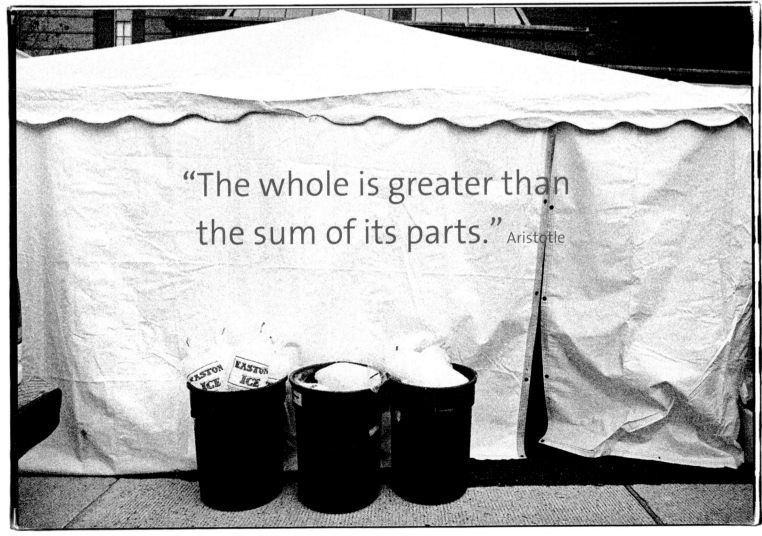

"The whole is greater than the sum of its parts." Aristotle

reimagining
the future
LEAFING OUT

Chez Panisse has always welcomed imaginative and talented young eccentrics into our family. Some of them are children of employees who grow up here and then pursue professional careers elsewhere. Others may arrive, stay for a while, and then launch interesting businesses of their own. Others may spark an unexpected renewal of Chez Panisse from within, go away to do something completely different, and return after a few years with new ideas and fresh ambitions. Still others pursue dual careers while working here. A chronicle of all the remarkable people who have worked here is way beyond the scope of this book. But it seems fitting to name at least a few members of the younger Panisse generations, if only to give an idea of the range of talent and inventiveness that we somehow are still able to nurture. Asiya Wadud (*left*), who has bartended in the Café and studied sociology, started a wonderful urban fruit bartering network called Forage Oakland. She began by pedaling around on her bicycle and knocking on strangers' doors when she spotted, say, a Persian mulberry tree with unharvested, ripening fruit. Now there is an informal network in place so that people in the East Bay can sign up to harvest and share backyard fruit with each other, fostering neighborliness, redistributing excess resources, and avoiding waste. Oliver Monday (*right*), is one of Sharon Jones's sons. Both Oliver and his brother, Nico, have worked at the restaurant. Nico (who has become, among other things, an expert in building outdoor ovens) is running a seasonal restaurant in Gloucester, Massachusetts, and Oliver has been helping him by contributing his formidable foraging skills. Oliver understands from the inside out both the practical and the philosophical connections between farm and table.

OLIVER MONDAY *(forager, philosopher)*: Growing up around the restaurant, I found myself wandering into the walk-in stuffed with boxes of produce, sneaking tastes. I knew one of Alice's key ideas was that great cooking starts with great ingredients—but what made this stuff the best? And where did it all come from?

I began to find answers after I graduated from college, when I spent a summer with Alice's friend Darina Allen and her family in County Cork, Ireland—a magical, transformative experience. I came to know what it is to live in close contact with the land and to directly nourish yourself and your community with the fruits of your labor. I discovered incredible joy— an elation that led me to Bob Cannard.

Bob is at once a teacher, philosopher, doctor, scientist, steward, chef, and, of course, a farmer. Perhaps being a farmer means being a bit of all of those things. He is by far the most generous person I have ever met, and it is clear that this quality stems from the generosity he experiences from nature—a generous blessing that is there for all, so long as we accept it. Having faith in the natural process, he always says, is the foundation from which human activity ought to spring forth. This trust is marked by humble acceptance of our relationship to the land and to one another, and gives us the confidence to approach and embrace the unknown free from timidity. Attempts to control and dominate are futile and ultimately degrade and diminish us. We must be willing and unafraid to make mistakes and, more importantly, to learn from them. Nature is incredibly generous, especially with its lessons! And so, too, should we be.

I am sitting on the porch at the home farm in Sonoma, watching a family of quail peck through the rocket patch. A heron slowly steps and bobs just beyond the rosemary hedge, across the road and on through the upland cress, savory, and thyme. Wild turkeys gobble in the forest up the hillside. The creek is full again after another spate of spring rain. The fruit trees have budded and blossomed and are now leafing out, as are the oaks. There is a thriving ecosystem here, and growing vegetables is only one portion of it. Everyone must eat, or else no one will.

Aha! The heron was on the hunt. A nice fat gopher speared and slung down its throat. I thought I was alone, but I turn my head and there is Bob, a few feet away (snuck up on me as usual), grinning ear to ear, eyes vibrant, and I know there is much to discuss.

Over the years I have been lucky to find young assistants who have been more calm, more affable, more clever, and more artistic than I could ever have hoped for. Varun Mehra, who began as my assistant in 2008, is a perfect example, an NYU graduate in business with great intuition.

VARUN MEHRA *(Alice's assistant)*: One of my first days at Chez Panisse, I had a transformational experience with a pluot from Baifang Schell's garden. We passed one around our office meeting, each staff member taking a loud chomp, our chins dripping magenta. They went on the menu in the fruit bowl that very night. I was so moved to discover it was that easy. I arrived at Chez Panisse as an intern a month before the Slow Food Nation gathering in San Francisco. Like so many others, I couldn't contain my wide-eyed amazement. There were interns, apprentices, and volunteers in every corner of Chez Panisse—staging in the kitchen, helping Max Gill, our florist, with his flower arrangements; or, like me, volunteering in Alice's office. Many only stay for a day, a week, others for a month or two. Restaurants, cafés, and bakeries are often inspired by a stint in the kitchen or a simple visit to Bob Cannard's farm. Interns at The Edible Schoolyard have dreamt up creative projects to bring real food to unex-

pected places. From the letterpress menus to handmade copper lamps, there are myriad vocations beyond food to discover within its walls. Chez Panisse is not a school, but with all of its graduates around the world, it certainly functions like one. I learned as much gathered around a table, sharing a just-picked pluot in its perfect moment, with colleagues I now consider family, as I did in any classroom.

FROM LEFT: David Prior, Varun Mehra, Greta Caruso, and Fanny Singer.

Sylvan Mishima Brackett is a former assistant with an inspired Japanese pop-up kitchen business. During his years in my office he distinguished himself by his equanimity, his congeniality, and his design skills.

SYLVAN MISHIMA BRACKETT *(owner, Peko-Peko)*: Sometime in my early twenties, I discovered the pleasure of the Japanese *izakaya*. Roughly speaking, these are taverns: places to consume beer, sake, or *shochu* with food that's straightforward and well suited to drinking. I loved the salary men, drunk at the yakitori stands under the tracks near Tokyo's Shimbashi station and the tiny low-key spots where I first tasted horse (raw, with garlic and green onion) and fried fish cake (simmered in broth with hot mustard). At its best, the food is simply prepared with good ingredients and made as you watch: a few pieces of mackerel sashimi with ginger, a rolled omelet made juicy with lots of dashi and *mirin*, a whole grilled *sanma*, fresh

enough to leave the guts in, with grated daikon.

I've translated my enthusiasm for the *izakaya* to the Bay Area. I've driven all over, hunting down ingredients. I've dug up bamboo shoots popping out of the ground in suburban backyards; skewered locally raised pastured chicken (heart, skin, and all) to grill as yakitori; fried up petrale sole caught the same day and eaten whole with bones and fins; pickled just-picked, tender red turnips and their leaves; cured steelhead salmon roe with soy and sake; and cooked freshly harvested California *koshihikari* rice. These days I find myself working in a little stall late at night, frying up gyoza, surrounded by drunk friends happily eating.

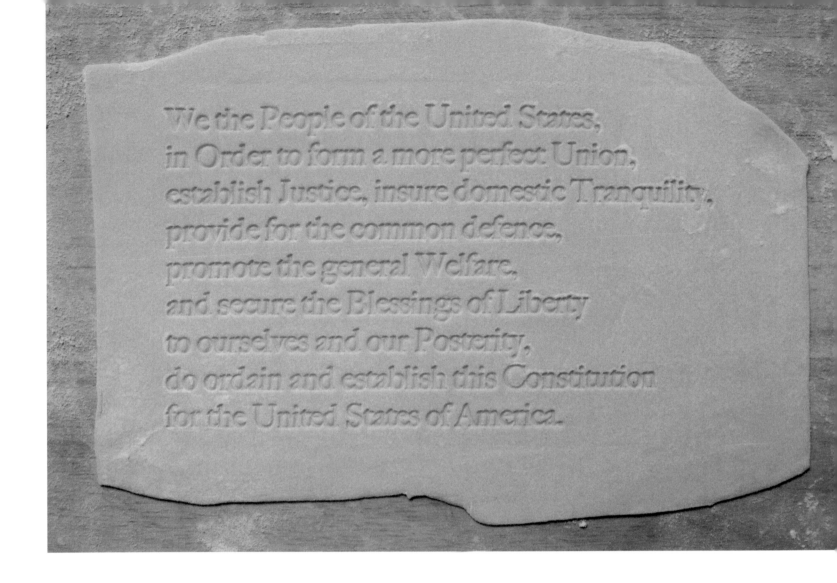

we the people

Jérôme Waag has a long history with the restaurant: his mother, Nathalie, is an old friend who was a formative influence on my earliest days in the kitchen, and he is now the downstairs chef in charge of the Monday-night menus. He is also a painter and a performance artist whose work explores, among other things, the ways in which food and culture meet and influence each other.

JÉRÔME WAAG *(artist, chef)*: *The Flavor of Democracy* is a performance piece centered around the making of a pasta I call *vespuccini*. *Vespuccini* are made by embossing the preamble to the Constitution of the United States into a sheet of fresh pasta dough and cutting it into strips along the lines of text. The audience participates in the making and cooking of the pasta, once they have come up with the ingredients for a sauce through a democratic decision-making process. *The Flavor of Democracy* was first performed with the artist Chris Sollars in the kitchen at his experimental performance space 667 Shotwell in San Francisco.

SAM WHITE *(artist, host)*: The spectacle of spit-roasting a 650-pound steer as part of OPENfuture (a reimagining of Futurist cuisine presented in conjunction with the San Francisco Museum of Modern Art) affected everyone differently. Vegetarians decided to try meat for the first time, and meat eaters felt they couldn't eat beef again. The art became a living, shared experience that redefined what something like beef can mean. OPENrestaurant is an artist group that sculpts food experiences to get lost in and learn from. Participants may be invited to pedal a bike that churns the ice cream for dessert or find where the tomatoes in the salad are from on an Oakland city map. Suddenly an image of the farmer who grew the greens you are eating is projected on the wall. The smell of the soil that they grew out of is in your glass, and the plants themselves are literally coming up out of the gallery floor. We take the framework of what a restaurant experience is known to be and bend it. We all speak the language of restaurants and use this platform to deepen the understanding of our relationship to food.

Sam White is a bartender and a host in the Café. Sam, Jérôme, and Stacie Pierce, one of our pastry chefs, are the prime movers of the OPENrestaurant collective, which, by displacing restaurant work into an art space, seeks to turn food preparation into a medium for artistic expression, often in unexpected and provocative ways.

Charlie Hallowell is one of the more recent alumni of our kitchens who have left to start marvelous restaurants of their own. He speaks for the scores of former Chez Panisse employees who continue to work in restaurants and other food businesses and who continue to believe in the nobility and righteousness of what we do.

CHARLIE HALLOWELL *(restaurateur, Pizzaiolo):* At Chez Panisse I learned how a restaurant can be much more than just a restaurant. I got a taste of how powerful a small local business can be, how many lives it can affect, how many stories can play out under one roof. At my restaurant I intended from the start to be an emissary of Alice's larger agenda, bringing her vision—of a return to the table and to older ways of connecting to the human beings around us—back to places that had lost sight of it. In these high-tech times, I am so grateful to stand in front of the wood-fired oven with my mortar and pestle and look out at my extended family of workers and customers eating and drinking and tapping their feet to the music while their children visit the chickens or play bocce. I think we have created spaces where people can let down their guard and come together as human beings, forgetting the stress of modern life and the stream of messages telling them they are not adequate or lovable, and remembering that they are divine children of this amazing world coming together to participate in the oldest ritual of all. Dinner!

Paris celebrated the Year of Biodiversity in May 2010 with a magical transformation: the Champs-Élysées was turned into a vast demonstration farm installed by the young farmers' union of France. It attracted two million visitors. I felt a surge of hope when I heard that its organizers want to take their concept worldwide.

JEFFREY BERG (*chairman and CEO, International Creative Management*): Dear Alice, I just got back from the Cannes Film Festival. I'm in Paris on the way back from Cannes. The entire Champs-Élysées has been converted into a mile-long garden filled with trees, fruits, vegetables, and flora from across the nation. The city of Paris has staged this event, and it is spectacular. Quite unlike anything I have seen after forty years in the film business. The boulevard is a complete botanical courtyard—top to bottom. The city also conscripted all the major local and national firms to assist in sponsorship.

The event is billed as "La Nature Capitale," and when this is written about in the world press, France will be celebrated, once again, for its progressive stance on the environment and how it plays a key role in urban life.

But the real theme is this: France is celebrating its young farmers as national heroes. In fact, as rock stars. The message is: *L'agriculture est capitale pour les générations future.* I'm returning home tomorrow but had to send this to you. Yours, Jeff

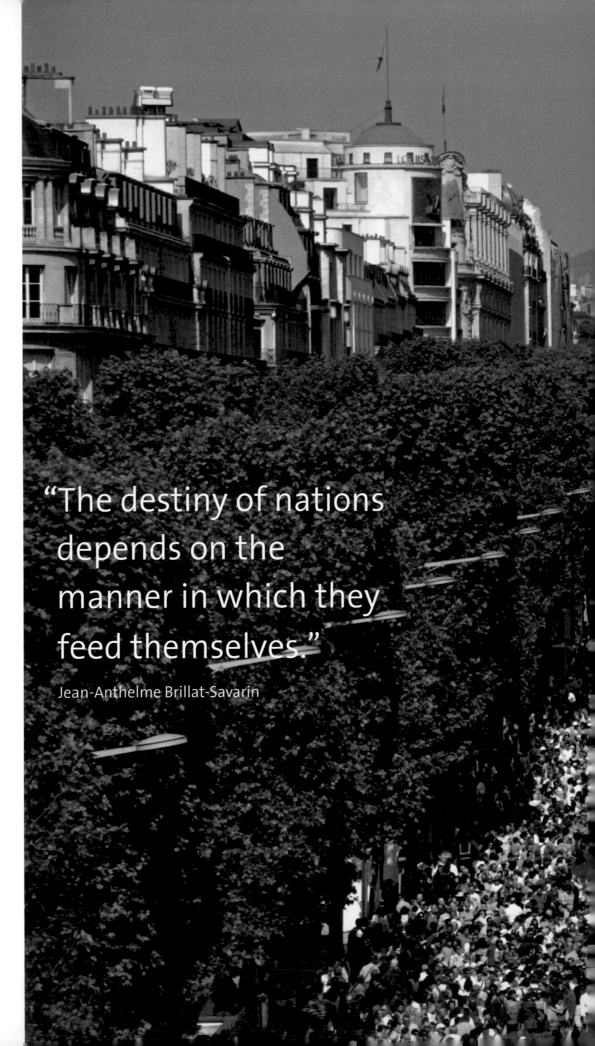

"The destiny of nations depends on the manner in which they feed themselves."

Jean-Anthelme Brillat-Savarin

I can tell it's May in this photograph because the cooks are shelling fava beans at their meeting. I'm sure that elsewhere around the restaurant, everyone else is shelling them, too— the people at their desks answering the phones, even the customers who come up to the bar are invited to join in. It's these everyday tasks that tie us together and let us know where we are in time and place.

FRITZ STREIFF (*former maître d'hôtel*): A magnificent evergreen tree with a beautiful dome-shaped crown has always towered over Chez Panisse. Ask what it is and you will probably be told it's a monkey-puzzle tree. It's not. It belongs to the same genus, but it's an *Araucaria bidwillii*, a bunya-bunya tree, also known as a false monkey-puzzle tree or a bunya pine. It is native to Australia; its name is indigenous Australian.

Our bunya-bunya was planted at least a hundred years ago and was already a mature tree by 1971. In the decades since, the tree has been cared for by Steve Crumley, who is an arborist as well as the longtime maître d'hôtel of the Café. Only Alice has worked at Chez Panisse longer than Steve, and only by a few months. The tree has required much care: the branchlets that form in clusters at the ends of its long, drooping branches bear leaves that are extremely sharp, so branches in the lower part of the tree have to be removed, and we have to pick up the branchlets brought down by the wind right away—while wearing gloves.

More dangerous than the leaves, however, are the seed-bearing cones, which are bigger and heavier than pineapples. The tree usually bears cones at three-year intervals (although some may form any year), and unless cut from the tree, they will fall, whole, which could cause injury to unlucky passersby. So Steve routinely climbs the tree to remove immature cones.

The thumb-size pine nuts in these cones are edible and considered choice by Australian bush-food enthusiasts. They were prized by indigenous Australians, to whom the bunya-bunya was sacred. The cone harvest every three years was the occasion for great ceremonial feasts when neighboring tribal groups would gather to sing, dance, trade goods, arrange marriages, resolve disputes, and draw strength from Mother Earth. It is fitting, is it not, that we gather at Chez Panisse for all the same purposes? One final, remarkable, relevant fact: bunya-bunyas can live over six hundred years.

under a spreading

bunya-bunya tree

40

Chez Panisse

ripeness is all

Afterword by Michael Pollan

MICHAEL POLLAN (*writer*): I arrived at the party that is Chez Panisse fairly late in its history, sometime during its fourth decade. My first meal at the restaurant, upstairs in the Café, came during the late spring or early summer of 2001, and a decade later, I cannot tell you what I had for dinner. It might have been the salmon, which at the time were still running not far outside the Golden Gate. The only thing I really remember from that meal was not a dish exactly, at least nothing cooked, though it did appear on the menu. It was, very simply, a bowl of fruit—some peaches. The menu gave the name of the farmer and the variety, neither of which meant anything to me at the time. But figuring those peaches had to be something pretty special to earn a spot on that menu—and to command a price only a dollar or two shy of the profiteroles and galette—I ordered it for dessert, not quite sure whether a plain bowl of fruit on a restaurant menu was best interpreted as an expression of culinary modesty or culinary audacity.

What arrived at the table was a small, unpolished bowl of hammered copper set atop a round, hammered copper base, and in that bowl rested two perfect peaches wreathed in a scatter of equally perfect raspberries. But by "perfect" I don't just mean perfect-looking, like a picture of fruit in a painting or magazine, though they were that, too: blushing, downy, plumped with juice. No, this was the higher perfection Ralph Waldo Emerson had in mind when he wrote, in reference to a very different fruit, "There are only ten minutes in the life of a pear when it is perfect to eat." In the case of a peach, that window is probably closer to seven minutes, and in the case of raspberries, maybe five. The wonder of it was that the kitchen had somehow arranged for those peaches and raspberries to land on our table not a moment sooner or later than that narrow interlude of perfection.

At the risk of offending the restaurant's many gifted chefs, that unadorned bowl of unimproved fruit strikes me as the essence of Chez Panisse, captures the restaurant's philosophy in a copper bowl. Since it first appeared on the menu in 1991, the fruit bowl has been Alice Waters's wordless way of saying that the true genius behind her food resides in the farmers who grew it and the breeders who bred it; the chef merely celebrates that genius by seizing on the moment of moments and setting it off between the quotation marks of a dish. Which is why the menu goes to the trouble of informing us that that the peach is a Sun Crest, the pear a Warren, and the tiny tangerine a kishu. There are times, the kitchen is saying, when no amount of culinary artifice can improve on what nature has already perfected, and it would be folly—hubris!—to try.

Not that there isn't a kind of genius in selecting that perfect peach or pear or tangerine. Samantha Greenwood, who worked in pastry back when the fruit bowl made its first appearance, remembers the hours spent sorting through bushel baskets looking for the Elect—a few dozen peaches worthy of the copper bowl. On the days when she couldn't find enough, the fruit bowl simply fell off the menu.

The fruit bowl is also a kind of timepiece, a way of marking the seasonal calendar, which is a rite that has always been central to the restaurant's project. When Churchill's kishus show up it must be late December; Swanton's strawberries say May, and the mulberries—the most fleeting fruit of all—signal the start of summer: somewhere around the third week of June. These moments remind us exactly where we are in the round of the year, or rather, where nature is. But try not to miss the moment of the mulberries, a fruit so fragile and ephemeral it's fallen completely out of commerce, except here on Shattuck Avenue on the very day they arrive. The mulberries, which come from a single tree in Sonoma owned by a man named Hugh Byrne, perhaps best exemplify the restaurant's fierce devotion to the nick of time.

Okay, but is it cooking?

Some would say no; the rap in certain culinary circles is that what Chez Panisse does best more closely resembles inspired shopping than inspired cooking. But I doubt that particular critique carries much of a sting in this particular kitchen. For Alice Waters's genius has been to show us there can be no inspired cooking without inspired shopping and, behind that, inspired farming. It's become a cliché of restaurant menus to mention farms, but Chez Panisse was the first to share bylines—pride of authorship—with the men and women who grow the food, recognizing that many of them are as gifted as any who have passed through the fabled kitchen. So we learn that the kishu was grown by Jim Churchill and Lisa Brenneis in Ojai, the Warren pear by Farmer Al at Frog Hollow Farm in Brentwood, and the Sun Crest peach by Mas Masumoto down near Fresno. The modesty of the fruit bowl consists in these acknowledgments.

But make no mistake, there is a certain audacity in play here too. It is the audacity of a Marcel Duchamp or Andy Warhol, artists who understood that sometimes the best art is found, not made. To pluck something out of the welter of the world and put a frame around it, or in this case a copper bowl, is a way of making us stop and pay attention, so that we might see the familiar with fresh eyes, and in this case not just eyes, but with every sense. Rightly seen, rightly tasted, the fruit bowl reminds us, the commonplace becomes miraculous.

Acknowledgments

This book took almost two years to put together, and it never would have happened without the eyes, energy, and artistry of Malgosia Szemberg. It was her unique vision to make this a picture book. She tirelessly designed and redesigned the thousands of components you see within these pages.

Fritz Streiff, the indispensable collaborator on all of my books, provided his remarkably nuanced conceptual, editorial, and creative support.

Bob Carrau patiently managed communications for the entire team and brought his essential skills as an artist and writer.

David Liittschwager and Sherry Olsen made sure all the images looked their best, while Spike Lomibao's digital design skills and way with type kept everything flowing.

Invaluable as reference and inspiration were Thomas McNamee's history of the restaurant and Carolyn Federman and Matt Jervis's photo book commemorating the thirty-fifth anniversary.

The prints and designs of both Patricia Curtan and David Goines have defined Chez Panisse over the years and their generosity to the restaurant cannot be overstated.

I am very grateful to all of my dear friends who helped, each in his own unique fashion, to bring this enormous project to completion—Eleanor Bertino, Sylvan Mishima Brackett, Susie Tompkins Buell and Mark Buell, Greta Caruso, Mark Danner, Angelo Garro, Samantha Greenwood, Marsha Guerrero, Doug Hamilton, Katrina Heron, Sharon Jones, Christina Kim, Tom Luddy, Greil Marcus, David McCormick, Varun Mehra, Cristina Mueller, Davia Nelson, Tony Oltranti, Cristina Salas-Porras, David Prior, Peter Sellars, Charles and Lindsey Shere, Jennifer Sherman, Fanny Singer, Gail Skoff, Craig St. John, Emily Takoudes, and Alta Tingle.

Finally, I'd like to thank our longtime customers and supporters: the wonderful patrons who have been part of the restaurant since it opened. This history is theirs as much as it is mine.

Contributors

JOHN ADAMS, the Pulitzer Prize–winning composer, has lived in Northern California since 1971. His works include five stage collaborations with director Peter Sellars, among them the Christmas oratorio *El Niño* and the opera *Nixon in China*.

COLMAN ANDREWS is the cofounder and former editor in chief of *Saveur* magazine. He is the author of *The Country Cooking of Ireland* and *Catalan Cuisine*, among other books.

BETSEY APPLE was married to R.W. Apple Jr., the *New York Times* chief correspondent and associate editor, and accompanied him on his gastronomic and enological researches.

JEFFREY BERG is the chairman and CEO of International Creative Management, the talent and literary agency.

WENDELL BERRY, the Kentucky farmer, poet, novelist, and cultural and economic critic, has written more than fifty books. Like five generations of his forebears, he farms in Henry County with a team of horses.

ELEANOR BERTINO was a maître d'hôtel at Chez Panisse before establishing her own San Francisco public relations firm. She has served on the boards of many organizations, including Slow Food USA.

PAUL BERTOLLI is the author of *Chez Panisse Cooking* and *Cooking by Hand*. In 2006, after ten years as chef at Chez Panisse and ten years as chef and co-owner of Oliveto, he founded his salumi business, Fra' Mani, and a food consulting company, Agrodolce, Inc.

SYLVAN MISHIMA BRACKETT was an assistant to Alice and a creative director at Chez Panisse before launching his Japanese-food catering company and pop-up *izakaya* restaurant, Peko-Peko.

MARK BUELL is a philanthropist and a former private and public housing developer in the Bay Area. He is board chairman of the Chez Panisse Foundation, president of the San Francisco Recreation and Park Commission, and a bread baker.

SUSIE TOMPKINS BUELL cofounded the Esprit clothing label and is now an activist and philanthropist who serves on the advisory board of the Chez Panisse Foundation. Her own foundation is devoted to promoting leadership among women and girls.

ADELE CHATFIELD-TAYLOR has been the president of the American Academy in Rome since 1988. She was awarded the 2010 Vincent Scully Prize for her work in historical preservation and arts administration.

SALLY CLARKE opened her London restaurant, Clarke's, in 1984. She is also the owner and proprietor of a provisions shop and a bakery, and the author of a cookbook, *Sally Clarke's Book*.

ESTHER COOK is a chef, storyteller, and educator. She has been the chef teacher of The Edible Schoolyard in Berkeley since the kitchen classroom's first year in 1997.

PATRICIA CURTAN is the artist and former Chez Panisse cook known for her design of the restaurant's menus and books, some of which she has coauthored. Her linocuts of mostly edible plants are widely collected and have been reproduced on calendars and wine labels and as notecards and tattoos.

MARK DANNER is a journalist, writer, and professor who has covered American foreign policy and international conflict for *The New Yorker* and *The New York Review of Books*. His most recent book is *Stripping Bare the Body: Politics Violence War*.

CAROLYN FEDERMAN is an event director and the producer in charge of Chez Panisse's fortieth birthday celebration, as she was for its thirtieth. Until 2009 she was also the director of development for the Chez Panisse Foundation.

ANYA FERNALD is an activist for sustainable food businesses and the founder of Oakland's Eat Real festival. She was the executive director of Slow Food Nation in 2008.

DAVID LANCE GOINES is a graphic artist, calligrapher, and the founder of Saint Hieronymus Press. His books include *The Free Speech Movement: Coming of Age in the 1960s* and *Punchlines: How to Start a Fight in Any Bar in the World*.

SAMANTHA GREENWOOD, a former cook in the pastry department and the Café, is now a special events chef for Chez Panisse. She is the 2010 world champion of the World Kettlebell Club's women's biathlon event.

MARSHA GUERRERO is the director of The Edible Schoolyard at Martin Luther King, Jr., Middle School in Berkeley. Before 2000, she worked in Singapore developing a coffee company and in San Francisco directing the operations of restaurant groups.

CHARLIE HALLOWELL is a former Café cook and pizzaiolo at Chez Panisse who now operates two Oakland restaurants, Pizzaiolo and Boot and Shoe Service, over one of which he lives in an apartment with his two children.

ANN HAMILTON is a visual artist known for her site-responsive installations. She has won many honors, including a MacArthur Fellowship and the Heinz Award, and has created major collaborative works for museums and institutions worldwide.

DOUG HAMILTON is a writer, director, and producer of documentary films, among them Emmy Award–winning episodes of the PBS series *Frontline*.

JAY HEMINWAY, sculptor and winemaker, and his wife, Pam, an artist, are the owners of Green & Red Vineyard in the Napa Valley. Their Zinfandel has been a signature red wine for Chez Panisse for decades.

KATRINA HERON is a journalist who has been editor in chief of *Wired* magazine and a senior editor at *Vanity Fair, The New Yorker,* and *The New York Times Magazine.* She was chairman of the board of Slow Food Nation in 2008 and serves on the board of the Chez Panisse Foundation.

ANNE ISAAK, a former Chez Panisse cook, has been a New York restaurateur (Elio's and Petaluma) for almost thirty years.

PAUL JOHNSON is the owner the Monterey Fish Market in Berkeley and the author of *Forever Fish.* He serves on the advisory board of the Monterey Bay Aquarium's Seafood Watch program.

SHARON JONES was a teacher of English as a second language at the University of California at Berkeley for more than twenty-five years. She currently serves on the board of directors of Chez Panisse.

KELSIE KERR is a writer and cooking teacher based in Berkeley. She is a former Chez Panisse chef and the co-author of Alice's recent cookbooks.

CHRISTINA KIM is an artist and the owner of dosa, the Los Angeles clothing and housewares line known for its fair-labor practices, incorporation of recycled materials, and international collaborations with traditional craftspeople and artisans.

NILOUFER ICHAPORIA KING is an anthropologist, kitchen botanist, and the author of *My Bombay Kitchen,* a book of Parsi home cooking. She lives in San Francisco with her husband, David King, and their parrot, Ordle.

PEGGY KNICKERBOCKER is a San Francisco–based cooking teacher and food writer. She is a longtime consulting editor of *Saveur* magazine and the author of five cookbooks. She was the curator of the olive oil pavilion at Slow Food Nation.

DIETER KOSSLICK, the director of the Berlin International Film Festival, was one of Slow Food's first members in Germany.

SIBELLA KRAUS is the president and founder of SAGE (Sustainable Agriculture Education), which works in support of sustainable regional food economies. While director of CUESA (Center for Urban Education in Sustainable Agriculture), she developed the San Francisco Ferry Plaza Farmers' Market.

CORBY KUMMER is a food writer in Boston, Massachusetts. He is a senior editor and a columnist for *The Atlantic,* the curator of the magazine's food blog, and the author of *The Pleasures of Slow Food* and *The Joy of Coffee.*

CAMILLE LABRO is a food writer and gastronomical tour guide. She lives in Paris with her family.

SAM LEVIN was a high school freshman in 2007 when he cofounded Project Sprout, which created a student-run organic garden in his Massachusetts public school district that supplies produce to three cafeterias and the community's hungry and is a living classroom for students at all grade levels.

SEEN LIPPERT is a food writer and teacher who cooked at Chez Panisse before becoming a chef in New York City. She lives in Greenwich, Connecticut, with her husband, Fred Landman.

TOM LUDDY is a film producer and programmer. He is a former director of the Pacific Film Archive and has worked since 1979 with American Zoetrope as a director of special projects and producer. He is the codirector and cofounder of the Telluride Film Festival, now in its thirty-eighth year.

KERMIT LYNCH is a wine merchant and the author of *Adventures on the Wine Route* and *Inspiring Thirst.* The French government has named him both a Chevalier de l'Ordre du Mérite Agricole and a Chevalier de la Légion d'Honneur. He lives in Berkeley and Provence.

DEBORAH MADISON was a student at the San Francisco Zen Center for eighteen years. She worked at Chez Panisse before becoming the chef of Greens and the author of more than ten cookbooks. She lives in New Mexico with her husband, the artist Patrick McFarlin.

GREIL MARCUS, an early investor in Chez Panisse and a member of its board of directors, is a cultural historian and music journalist. His books include *Lipstick Traces: A Secret History of the 20th Century* and, most recently, *When That Rough God Goes Riding: Listening to Van Morrison.*

PATRICK MARTINS founded Slow Food USA in 2000. In 2004, he left to found Heritage Foods USA, an independent company that helps rescue vanishing foods and family farms by marketing products such as heritage breeds of turkey.

LAURA MASER, one of Alice's sisters, is an artist and a founder and owner of Café Fanny in Berkeley.

NICHOLAS MCGEGAN, the conductor and early music expert, is the music director of San Francisco's Philharmonia Baroque Orchestra and the artistic director of the Göttingen International Handel Festival. In 2010 he was appointed an Officer of the Order of the British Empire.

VARUN MEHRA, Alice's assistant, is a recent graduate of New York University, where he studied business.

JOHN MEIS is the author of *A Taste of Tuscany*, a cookbook about the region of Italy where he has long resided and where he works as a travel and cultural consultant and guide.

MARK MILLER is a restaurateur and food consultant based in Santa Fe, New Mexico, and the author of many cookbooks.

OLIVER MONDAY has studied philosophy and environmental studies and worked as a farmer and forager.

RUSSELL MOORE left Chez Panisse after twenty-one years to become the chef of Camino in Oakland, which he started with his wife, Allison Hopelain, in 2008.

KHALIL MUJADEDY is the maintenance director of Chez Panisse and a builder and craftsman whose work in copper is a feature of the restaurant's design. He lives in Pinole, California, with his wife, Palwasha, and their three children.

SUE MURPHY is a producer, writer, and stand-up comic. She won two Emmy awards for writing and producing *The Ellen DeGeneres Show* and is now co–executive producer of *Chelsea Lately*.

JOAN NATHAN is the author of ten cookbooks, including *Quiches, Kugels, and Couscous: My Search for Jewish Cooking in France*. She was guest curator of Food Culture USA at the 2005 Smithsonian Folklife Festival.

DAVIA NELSON is one of the Kitchen Sisters, the producers of award-winning National Public Radio documentary series, including *Hidden Kitchens, Lost & Found Sound,* and *The Hidden World of Girls*. She is also a casting director and screenwriter.

BRUCE NEYERS and his wife, Barbara, a former Chez Panisse maître d'hôtel and manager, are the proprietors of Neyers Vineyard. Bruce is also the national sales director of Kermit Lynch Wine Merchant.

TEDDY SZEMBERG O'CONNOR, a recent intern at the Rome Sustainable Food Project, is a student of engineering at Imperial College London.

SCOTT PEACOCK is a chef, writer, and food documentarian. He is the coauthor of *The Gift of Southern Cooking*, which he wrote with Edna Lewis, who he cared for until her death in 2006.

CAL PETERNELL has been a chef of the Chez Panisse Café for more than ten years. Before moving to the East Bay with his wife, the artist Kathleen Henderson, he pursued a career in art in Lucca, Italy.

CARLO PETRINI is the founder and president of the international Slow Food movement and cofounder of the University of Gastronomic Sciences in Bra, the city of his birth.

GILBERT PILGRAM started at Chez Panisse as a prep cook, becoming sous-chef and Café co-chef before taking over as general manager of the restaurant in 2000. He left in 2006 and is now co-owner, with Judy Rodgers, of the Zuni Café in San Francisco.

MICHAEL POLLAN is a food activist, journalist, and the author of *The Omnivore's Dilemma* and *In Defense of Food*. Since 2003 he has been the John S. and James L. Knight Professor of Journalism at UC Berkeley's Graduate School of Journalism.

DAVID PRIOR is a travel and food writer and the communications director for the Chez Panisse Foundation.

CLARE PTAK was a Chez Panisse cook before moving to London, where she founded Violet, a baking company, café, and cake shop. She is the author of *The Whoopie Pie Book*.

RUTH REICHL, the former restaurant critic of the *New York Times* and editor in chief of the former magazine *Gourmet*, is the author and editor of several cookbooks and the author of four volumes of memoir.

CRISTINA SALAS-PORRAS was an assistant to Alice for nine years and is now a creative consultant to food and hospitality businesses in the United States and Japan.

ORVILLE SCHELL is the former dean of the Graduate School of Journalism at UC Berkeley, and the Arthur Ross Director of the Center on U.S.-China Relations at the Asia Society in New York. Among his books not about China is *Modern Meat: Antibiotics, Hormones, and the Pharmaceutical Farm*.

ERIC SCHLOSSER is a journalist who has investigated the war on drugs and the prison system as well as our industrial food system. He is the author of *Fast Food Nation: The Dark Side of the All-American Meal* and the producer of the documentary *Food, Inc.*

PETER SELLARS is a teacher and a theater, opera, and festival director whose work challenges conventional expectations of the social and political role of the performing arts. He has won the Erasmus Prize and the Gish Prize.

CHARLES SHERE is a composer and writer. He maintains two blogs: *The Eastside View* and *Eating Every Day*. Both he and his wife, Lindsey Remolif Shere, who was the restaurant's pastry chef for more than twenty-five years, are among the owners of Chez Panisse.

JENNIFER SHERMAN cooked in the Chez Panisse downstairs kitchen in the nineties, left to work as a private chef and consultant for several years, and returned to become general manager in 2008.

FANNY SINGER, the daughter of Alice and Stephen Singer, lives in England, where she is a doctoral candidate in the history of art at the University of Cambridge.

MARK SINGER is a staff writer at *The New Yorker* and Alice's former brother-in-law. His books include *Funny Money* and *Somewhere in America*.

STEPHEN SINGER is a restaurateur, a former wine retailer, and the owner and proprietor of Baker Lane Vineyards, a Sonoma winemaking venture, and Stephen Singer Olio, an olive oil and vinegar importing business. He and Alice were married for many years.

PEGGY SMITH, former Chez Panisse Café chef, is a founder and owner of Cowgirl Creamery, an organic cheesemaking and artisanal cheese retailing venture based in Point Reyes Station, with shops in San Francisco and Washington, D.C.

FRITZ STREIFF was a cook, bartender, and maître d'hôtel at Chez Panisse for almost twenty years. He has been Alice's literary collaborator for thirty. He lives in Hong Kong.

STEVE SULLIVAN is a baker and former Chez Panisse busboy. He is the founder and president of the Berkeley-based Acme Bread Company.

MONA TALBOTT became the first director of the Rome Sustainable Food Project at the American Academy in 2007 after a career at Chez Panisse and as a private chef. She is coauthor of *Biscotti*, the first of a series of single-subject cookbooks from the Academy's kitchen.

ALAN TANGREN trained as a meteorologist before working at Chez Panisse as a chef and forager for twenty-five years. Since 2006 he has farmed his family's old orchard in the Sierra foothills.

DAVID TANIS, the co-chef of Chez Panisse, spends half the year in Berkeley and the rest in Paris, New York, and elsewhere. His most recent book is *Heart of the Artichoke and Other Kitchen Journeys*.

STEPHEN THOMAS, an artist and teacher, is the founding director of the Oxbow School, an interdisciplinary one-semester boarding school for high school students with a strong inclination toward the visual arts. He is married to Patricia Curtan.

CALVIN TRILLIN, the journalist, novelist, memoirist, essayist, and comic poet born in Kansas City, is a staff writer for *The New Yorker* and the author of more than twenty books. He lives in Greenwich Village.

PATRICIA UNTERMAN is a San Francisco restaurant critic and food writer and the chef and co-owner of the Hayes Street Grill.

JOSH VIERTEL has been the president of Slow Food USA since 2008. He was a teacher and organic farmer before cofounding the Yale Sustainable Food Project, which he codirected for six years.

JÉRÔME WAAG is an artist who also cooks at Chez Panisse, where he is Monday-night downstairs chef. His work has included performances and installations at the Headlands Center for the Arts in Marin County and at the Global Art Lab in Osh, Kyrgyzstan.

BOB WAKS is a nurse who lives in Berkeley. He was an original member of the Cheese Board collective and a sous-chef at Chez Panisse in its earliest days.

SARAH WEINER was an assistant to Alice and served as content director for Slow Food Nation 2008. She is the founder and executive director of Seedling Projects, which presents the Good Food Awards.

JACQUELINE WEST is a costume designer who has been nominated twice for the Oscar for Best Costume Design. In the 1980s she operated her own clothing store in Berkeley next door to Chez Panisse.

SAM WHITE is an artist in Oakland who works as a host and bartender at Chez Panisse.

FAITH WILLINGER is a cook, teacher, and writer who has spent more than thirty years in the study of Italian food and wine. Her books include the guidebook *Eating in Italy* and *Adventures of an Italian Food Lover*. She lives in Florence with her Tuscan husband.

Credits

To assemble this book we sorted through a blizzard of photographs that came at us from many different directions. We have made every effort to identify and credit as many of the photographers as we can, and we apologize to those who remain unidentified because of error, forgetfulness, and the passage of time. We thank the credited and uncredited alike for their distinctive and invaluable contributions to this book.

Nick Allen: 55 (center); Associated Press: (1964 file photo) 17; Arlene Bernstein: 53 (bottom); Richard Beveridge: 29; Les Blank/lesblank.com: 54, 55 (all except center); Jeff Bordes/Frog Hollow Farm: 169; Darryl Bush/San Francisco Examiner: 114 (bottom left); Aya Brackett: 103, 141 (peaches in jar), 148, 186, 200 (top left, top right), 210, 230–31, 241, 262, 263, 264, 265, 282 (bottom four), 288–89, 291, 294; Bob Buechler: 141 (top left); Roberto Caccuri/Contrasto/Redux: 252–53, 254–55, 256, 257; Bob Carrau: 66 (top), 94, 107, 132, 141 (all color images except peaches in jar), 142–43, 198, 199, 200 (David Tanis peeling apples, David Tanis writing menu), 218, 219, 220, 221 (top, second from bottom), 236, 237; Constance Chatfield-Taylor: 246, 247, 248 (top left), 248–49; Ina Chun: 68; Tasha DeSerio: 98 (top); James DiLoreto (courtesy of the Smithsonian): 229 (row 3, left); Daidie Donnelley: 93 (top right); Colin Drake: 179, 180–81, 182, 183, 184, 185, 191 (bottom right), 192, 193, 194–95, 196, 197; Andrew Dunkely and Marcus Leith (courtesy of the artist; neugerriemschneider, Berlin, and Tanya Bonakdar Gallery, New York): 217 (The Weather Project, 2003, by Olafur Eliasson; Turbine Hall, Tate Modern, London; monofrequency lights, projection foil, haze machines, mirror foil, aluminum, and scaffolding; 26.7m x 22.3m x 155.4m); Faith Echtermeyer: 115, 116; Randy Fertel: 239 (center); Sean Fraga: 222, 223; Full Belly Farm: 64–65; Sam Fuller: 281; Thomas John Gibbons: 208; Warren

Charles Goines: 24; Maureen Gosling: 54 (top right), 86–87, 88, 89, 95 (top left); Samantha Greenwood: 66 (bottom), 67 (top), 70, 150; Ann Hamilton: 211; Doug Hamilton: 224, 225, 227, 228, 229 (all except row 3, left), 234 (top), 242–43, 245, 250–51, 275; Pamela Hatchfield: 244 (top); John Hill: 146 (top) Suki Hill: 203; Christopher Hirsheimer: 122, 123, 124, 125, 276, 277, 278, 279; Eiko Ishioka: 126–27, 129, 130; Daphne Johnson/Lucidpics Photography: 134; Maira Kalman: 145; Catherine Karnow: 105 (bottom); Robert Kusel/Lyric Opera of Chicago: 214 (bottom); Brigitte Lacombe: 8; Enrique Laroche: 28; Annie Leibovitz: 155, 170; David Liittschwager: 160, 162, 163, 231 (top right), 234 (six color images); Mariquita Farm: 69; Duke and Joyce McGillis: 82; Robert Messick: 47, 56 (bottom left, bottom right), 90–91, 92–93, 96, 97, 99, 100–101, 111, 112, 114 (bottom right), 138 (black-and-white image), 139 (top), 152 (all except bottom left), 174; James Monday: 109; Sue Murphy: 282 (top); Jill Norman and the Estate of Elizabeth David (courtesy of): 118; Teddy Szemberg O'Connor: 272–73; Ene Osteraas-Constable: 232; Office of Charlie Chaplin: 55 (center); Michael Palmieri: 212; Paramount Pictures: 292 (still image from the film *Marius*, 1931); Lynn Persin: 216; Lulu Peyraud (courtesy of): 77; Claire Ptak: 273; San Francisco Chronicle: 146 (bottom); Stuart Ramson/The Sundance Channel: 213; Sara Remington: 280; Dan Rest/Lyric Opera of Chicago: 214 (top three); Charles Shere: 36–37, 41, 48, 50 (top), 59, 104, 105 (top); Gail Skoff: 51, 61, 71, 74, 75 (top left, bottom right), 76, 84, 114 (top), 121; Valerio Borgianelli Spina: 244 (bottom); Tommy Strück: 258–59, 260–61, 266, 268–69, 270, 271; Vern Sutcher: 136–37, 138 (color images), 139 (bottom); Malgosia Szemberg: 221 (second from top, bottom); Charles Villyard: 284; Jérôme Waag: 283; Nathalie Waag: 78–79, 80–81; Sam White: 285 (bottom); Phillipe Wojazer/Reuters: 286–87; Lora Zarubin: 188, 189, 190–91

Index

A watched pot

Somewhere between a sautoir
and a casserole russe,
somewhat short-handled,
with cover.

For Paul Bertolli and Alice Waters

—JOHN HOLLANDER

```
                              Not
                   to mark the first
                 dreaming slow whisper
      of steam soon to be too hot for silences to handle
                 but this still lidded form
                 hiding a troubled surface
                 within Boiling will sound
                 deep but hollow Only what
                 we have made makes scents
                 Not for us the mere water
                 falling away to what this
                 bottom can give rise to
```